EXPERIMENTING WITH
TIME

BY ROBERT GARDNER

A VENTURE BOOK
FRANKLIN WATTS
NEW YORK / CHICAGO / LONDON / TORONTO / SYDNEY

Photographs copyright ©: North Wind Picture Archives: p. 6; Archive Photos: pp. 13 (J. Jay Hirz), 31 (Lambert), 33 top, 93 (Lawrence Thornton), 113 (Ed Carlin); The Bettmann Archive: pp. 19, 40; Photo Researchers, Inc.: pp. 33 bottom (Stephen J. Krasemann), 48 (Allan Morton/SPL), 73 (Dr. Fred Espenak/SPL); Visuals Unlimited/Tom J. Ulrich: p. 37; Robert Gardner: pp. 55, 82, 95; Deutches Museum, Munchen: pp. 89, 98, 102, 105, 106, 114; National Maritime Museum, Greenwich, London: pp. 119, 125; Education Development Center, Inc.: p. 137; The Harold E. Edgerton 1992 Trust/Palm Press: p. 141.

Library of Congress Cataloging-in-Publication Division

Gardner, Robert, 1929–
Experimenting with time / by Robert Gardner.
    p. cm. — (A Venture book)
    Includes bibliographical references and index.
    ISBN 0-531-12554-8
    1. Time measurements—Experiments. 1.Title.
QB213.G37 1995
529'.7'078—dc20   95-1471
                                                        CIP

CONTENTS

INTRODUCTION

Time, like intelligence and energy, is more easily measured than defined. Early humans measured time in natural units—days, months, and years. A day was the time from one sunrise to the next. Because the time of sunrise changes, they later defined a day as the time between middays. Midday is when the Sun reaches the highest point in its daily path across the sky.

A month was the time between one full moon and the next. A year was the time for the Sun to shift its path from the highest midday position in the sky to the lowest and back again. That is the time from the longest day of the year (around June 20) to the shortest day of the year (around December 20) and back to the longest day.

With primitive clocks using shadows cast by the Sun, it became possible to divide the day into hours. Later, mechanical clocks led to the division of hours into minutes and minutes into seconds. Today, atomic

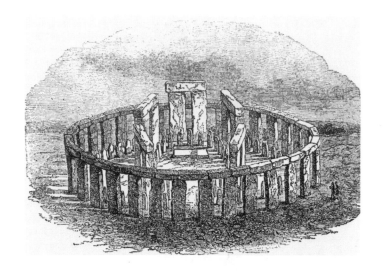

The early humans who built England's Stonehenge probably kept track of time according to the position of the Sun. Although its purpose is unknown, Stonehenge, shown here restored to the way it probably appeared in 1550 B.C., had an entryway that aligned with the sunrise on the summer solstice.

clocks measure time in units as small as nanoseconds (billionths of a second).

Being able to measure time does not mean we can define it. In fact, what we mean by time varies. We all perceive psychological time. Time spent on a boring task seems longer to most people than equal clock-time spent on something we enjoy. As we grow older, time seems to pass faster. This may be a matter of time ratios. For a 5-year-old, 1 year is one-fifth of all the time he or she has known. But a year is only 2 percent of the time a 50-year-old person has been alive.

The time measured by ordinary clocks is based on

the motion of the Sun relative to the Earth. You will see that it is different from the time astronomers use, called *sidereal time*. That's because astronomers are more interested in locating distant stars than the nearby Sun. You will also see that time depends on velocity. Clocks moving at high speeds tick less frequently than identical clocks at rest.

In the pages that follow, you'll find more than 50 investigations or projects that involve various aspects of time. As you might guess, there are experiments related to clocks, sun clocks, and star clocks, as well as mechanical clocks, quartz clocks, and atomic clocks. You'll learn how our concept of time has evolved, how time is used in establishing rates such as speed, and how people propose to change our current calendar, which is much different today than it was when Julius Caesar changed it more than 2,000 years ago. You'll investigate the important role time plays in our society and how even the temperature of our bodies changes during the course of a single day according to the rhythms of time. Investigations about time, like time itself, are never ending.

The level of difficulty of the investigations and projects varies. Some are quite straightforward and easy to do. Others are quite challenging and require careful preparation, thought, and analysis. However, you do not have to do all the experiments, nor do you have to do most of them in any particular order. Choose the ones that you find interesting, but keep in mind that you can learn a lot by choosing at least one or more investigations that challenge your mind and skills and require you to think deeply. Only by striving to understand those things that you find difficult can you develop your thinking and reasoning skills to their fullest. If you choose to meet such challenges, you'll find that your self-esteem will improve as much as your grasp of science and time.

Some investigations make use of metric units, which are widely used in science and in most countries throughout the world. In others, the English units are used because they will be more familiar to readers. Fortunately, both the metric and English systems of measurement use the same units of time—seconds, minutes, hours, days, and years. The following table contains all the units you will need. You may also find it useful in converting units within or between the metric and English systems.

Conversions for Units of Measurement Used in Experiments

Time and frequency (metric and English)

1.0 hour (h) = 60 minutes (min) = 3,600 seconds (s)
1.0 min = 60 s
1.0 Hz (hertz) = 1.0 change/s (e.g., 1.0 wave/s or
                         1.0 vibration/s)

Length

Metric	English
1.0 kilometer (km) = 1,000 meter (m)	1.0 mile (mi) = 1,760 yards (yd) = 5,280 feet (ft)

1.0 m = 100 centimeters (cm)	1.0 yd = 3.0 ft = 36 inches (in)
1.0 cm = 10 millimeters (mm)	1.0 ft = 12 in
Metric to English	*English to metric*
1.0 m = 3.28 ft = 1.09 yd	1.0 ft = 0.305 m = 30.5 cm
1.0 cm = 0.394 in	1.0 in = 2.54 cm = 0.0254 m
1.0 km = 0.62 mi	1.0 mi = 1.61 km

Speed or velocity

Metric	*English*
1.0 km/h (kmph) = 1,000 m/s	1.0 mi/h (mph) = 1.47 ft/s
1.0 m/s = 100 cm/s	1.0 ft/s = 12 in/s = 0.68 mph
Metric to English	*English to metric*
1.0 kmph – 0.62 mph	1.0 mph = 1.61 kmph
1.0 m/s = 1.09 yd/s = 3.28 ft/s	1.0 ft/s = 0.305 m/s = 30.5 cm/s

Volume

Metric	*English*
1.0 cubic meter (m^3) = 1,000,000 cubic centimeters (cm^3)	1.0 cubic yard (yd^3) = 27 cubic feet (ft^3)
1.0 liter (L) = 1,000 milliliters (ml)	1.0 ft^3 = 1,728 in^3
	1.0 gallon (gal) = 4.0 quarts (qt) = 231 in^3
Metric to English	*English to metric*
1.0 m^3 = 1.30 yd^3 = 35.3 ft^3	1.0 ft^3 = 0.028 m^3
1.0 cm^3 = 0 .061 in^3	1.0 in^3 = 16.4 cm^3

Conversions for Units of Measurement Used in Experiments (continued)

Mass

Metric
1.0 kilogram (kg) = 1,000 grams (g)

Force or weight

Metric	*English*

1.0 newton (N) =
    100,000 dynes (dyn)
	1.0 pound (lb) =
	    16 ounce (oz)

Metric to English 1.0 N = 0.22 lb	*English to metric* 1.0 lb = 4.45 N = 445,000 dyn

Work or energy

Metric	*English*

1.0 N x 1.0 m = 1.0 N–m
    = 1.0 joule (J)
	1.0 lb x 1.0 ft =
	    1.0 ft-lb

Metric to English 1.0 J = 0.74 ft-lb	*English to metric* 1.0 ft-lb = 1.36 J

TIME: A BEGINNING WITHOUT AN END?

Time is a common word in our vocabulary. A great variety of expressions pertain to time: "Time to rise and shine!" "Time out!" "Dinner time!" "Time on your hands." "There's no time like the present." How many other common phrases can you think of that contain the word *time*?

Psychologically, we perceive time as a continuum, or a continuous progression, along which a series of events take place. We are born; we learn to walk and talk; we start school; we learn to read; we enter middle school. We plant seeds; we watch the plants emerge from the soil, grow, bloom, and bear fruit; we harvest the fruit and gather seeds to plant the following spring. But does time exist apart from everything else?

Galileo was the first scientist to consider time an independent variable—that is, a quantity not tied to the changes of another variable. In carrying out his experiments on the motion of freely falling bodies, he compared the times it took a ball to roll different distances along an inclined grooved board. He found that the distance the ball moved was proportional to the square of the time. To measure the time, he used a water clock; his unit of time was the volume of water that flowed from the clock as the ball rolled along the board.

When the distance the ball rolled was quadrupled, the time for the ball to travel that distance was doubled; the volume of water flowing from the clock doubled. If the distance the ball traveled along the incline was increased by nine times, the time to travel that distance tripled; three times as much water flowed. (If you would like to repeat Galileo's experiment, see page 35 of my book *Famous Experiments You Can Do*, which is listed in the For Further Reading section at the back of this book.)

When Sir Isaac Newton developed a new view of the universe half a century after Galileo's death, he wrote, "Absolute, true, mathematical time, of itself, and from its own nature, flows equably (steadily) without relation to anything external."

Before Newton, time was believed to be tied to motion. Time existed only because of the motion of the stars and the Sun. It was the Sun, after all, that gave rise to the morning's light as it ascended into the eastern sky, and it was the Sun's disappearance below the western horizon each evening that led to the darkness of night. Calendars were developed to help people identify the time of religious holidays, prepare for planting and harvesting, and anticipate periods when rain might be expected. But calendars did not suggest a uniform, unending, regular flow of time.

This fourteenth-century timekeeper in the Cathedral of Lund in Sweden is called a horologe. The 24-hour dial was designed to represent the astronomical sky. In addition to indicating time according to the movements of the Sun, the moon, and the stars, the clock indicates the moon's phases and the position of the constellations of the zodiac.

In fact, the difficulty in finding a practical, exact, and workable calendar probably reinforced the notion that time depends on the motion of celestial bodies. Even the invention of clocks did not change our ancestors' concept of time as motion-dependent. Early clocks, which were accurate only to the nearest hour, served primarily as models of the solar system.

Our present concept of time arose between the twelfth and sixteenth centuries. Galileo did not invent the idea of time as a steady flow independent of motion. He simply adopted the idea because it gave him a better way to explain motion, particularly accelerated motion. It is quite likely that music gave rise to the modern concept of time. In writing polyphonic church music, in which several melodies are sung simultaneously, the composer and the singers had to be very much aware of ongoing time. Notation for indicating time durations—quarter notes, half notes, and full notes—was developed during this period. Because music was composed and sung independently of any celestial events or motion, it may have gradually changed the way humans regarded time.

TIME ZERO

Half a century ago, there were two competing theories about the universe. The steady state theory held that the universe is unchanging and has existed forever. Time had no beginning and will have no end. A second theory, now the prevailing one, is known as the Big Bang theory. The Big Bang is a huge explosion believed to have taken place some 15 to 20 billion years ago. As a result of the explosion, the theory goes, all the matter that makes up the universe began to fly outward in all directions.

The time the Big Bang occurred is so indefinite because recent observations by the Hubble Space Telescope indicate the universe is about 8 billion years old, whereas astronomers have observed stars that appear to be 16 billion years old. Clearly, some astronomical theories will have to be modified since the stars cannot be older than the universe.

Despite the discrepancy, astronomers have gathered an abundance of evidence indicating that the universe was born in this way and that it is still expanding. If this expansion continues, then time will continue without end. However, if the gravitational attraction of all the matter in the universe is strong enough to stop the expansion and pull the matter back together, there could be another Big Bang. Would time begin again? Or do we have yet another unit of time—the time from one Big Bang to the next?

Project 1

Assume that the Big Bang, which marks the beginning of the universe, took place about 20 billion years ago, and that our Sun, the Earth, and the other planets came into existence about 5 billion years ago. Primitive forms of life appeared on Earth about 3.5 billion years ago, and land animals have inhabited Earth for only the last 400 million years. Mammals did not appear until nearly 200 million years ago, and primates—the family of apes, monkeys, and humans—didn't appear for another 140 million years. The remains of primates who appear to be the ancestors of humans are 2 million years old, but people similar to us have probably been around for only about the last 100,000 years.

Draw a line representing time lengthwise along a sheet of wrapping or adding-machine paper at least a meter (yard) long. At the left end of the line make a mark representing the beginning of the universe. At the right end of the line make a mark representing the present, 20 billion years later. On your line, insert marks to indicate the (1) first primitive forms of life, (2) appearance of land animals, (3) first mammals, (4) presence of primates, (5) appearance of the ancestors of human beings, (6) presence of people similar to us.

You will probably need a second, shorter line to represent an expanded view of the last 2 million years of human evolution. There may not be room on the original line to mark accurately the last 100,000 years during which humans similar to us have inhabited the Earth. As you can see, humans appeared very recently on the time line of the universe. If you represent the age of the universe by 1 year, how long have humans been around? If you represent it by 1 day, how long have humans been here?

TIME
AND
LIFE

We are a very time-conscious society. "What time is it?" is one of the most common questions you hear because time plays an important role in daily life. You get up at a certain time each morning; go to a school that begins and ends at fixed times; eat your meals at the same times each day; agree to meet a friend at a certain place at a specific time; and turn on your favorite television programs at their scheduled times.

Investigation 1: Time in Our Lives

The purpose of this investigation is to give you a sense of the important role that time plays in your life. For an entire day, record every instance in which you look at a clock or watch, or ask someone what time it is. Make a check mark (✓) with a pen or pencil on a pocket-size notebook or a card each time you look at a timepiece or ask for the time. If the time check is essential, that is, if you really need to know what time it is in order to catch a bus, reach a class on time, be home for dinner, etc., make two check marks (✓✓).

Just before going to bed, count the total number of ✓'s and ✓✓'s in your record. How many time checks did you make? What fraction of your time checks were essential?

Ask a number of other people, including, if possible, people of different ages and occupations, to carry out the same experiment you did. After looking at their data, can you determine whether adults are more time conscious than children? Whether time consciousness is related to occupation?

As a society, we would be lost without clocks and watches. But how closely do these timepieces agree? Compare all the clocks and watches in your home. By how many seconds, minutes, or hours do they differ?

Compare your watch or clock with those of a few friends, with your school's clock, and with the clocks at banks and post offices. How closely do these clocks or watches agree with yours? How can you find the greatest time difference between any two of the timepieces you investigated?

CIRCADIAN RHYTHMS

Many of the common rhythms we experience in life were invented by humans. The tick-tock of a clock on the mantle, the repeated rings of a telephone, the red-yellow-green cycle of a traffic light, the dripping of a leaky faucet, and the back-and-forth motion of an automobile's windshield wipers are all examples of rhythms arising from human inventions. These time-related pat-

Morning glories open during the day and close at night in response to circadian rhythms.

terns did not exist before humans learned to develop and use tools.

Other time-related patterns found in nature are independent of a human presence. You may be aware of certain flowers, such as the morning glory, that open in the morning and close at night, of birds that awaken you with their songs at sunrise but are silent most of the day, of moths that fly at night, and their counterparts—butterflies—that fly in daylight and rest at night. Natural rhythms that occur on a 24-hour cycle are called *circadian rhythms.*

Circadian rhythms appear to have an innate source. Some kind of internal clock appears to regulate behavior. The leaves of plants placed in darkness continue to follow the same patterns of movement that they follow in normal sunlight. Birds kept under conditions of constant light and temperature continue to feed on a time schedule that is very similar to their feeding habits in a normal environment.

Many animals also appear to have circannual, or yearly, rhythms. In one experiment, ground squirrels were kept in a controlled environment that included plenty of food and water, a constant temperature of 0°C (32°F), and equal hours of light and darkness each day. Even without the cue of changing seasonal light, the squirrels would hibernate on schedule in the autumn. In the spring, their body temperatures and eating habits returned to normal as they emerged from hibernation, again on their normal annual cycle.

TIME AND PEOPLE

Most people's lives are based on a 24-hour cycle. Jobs, schools, trains, planes, buses, theaters, and radio and television programs are all based on schedules that force us to live by the clock. You might wonder how people managed to live before clocks were invented.

Suppose you were placed in dark, subterranean quarters illuminated only by artificial light with no clocks or watches. Would you continue to follow a circadian rhythm?

A number of experiments designed to answer that question have been performed. People were placed in closed, isolated quarters without timekeeping instruments for periods of three months or more. Their only contact to the outside was a single telephone line linking them to others involved in the experiment, whom they called when they went to bed, awakened, or ate.

Surprisingly, most of the subjects in such experiments gradually developed their own daily time cycle. The average was 25 hours. Their bedtimes, awakening times, and other daily activities were separated by 25 hours, on the average, not 24. But various people or groups of people developed different cycles—usually somewhere between 23 and 26 hours.

Although these experiments revealed that 24 hours is not a natural daily cycle for many people, almost everyone adjusts to the 24-hour cycle established by the Sun. What many find difficult is changing their sleeping habits from night to day as some jobs require. Another difficulty, though less onerous, is shifting their bedtime after rapid air travel over several time zones. This is known as jet lag.

Most people can adjust to jet lag after a day or two, but it may require several weeks to adjust to sleeping from 2 P.M. to 10 P.M. rather than from 10 P.M. to 6 A.M. Experiments with hamsters who were subjected to changes in light and dark cycles equivalent to a flight across eight time zones suggest that activity may be the key to overcoming jet lag. If the hamsters were kept active after the time change, they required only about 36 hours to adjust to the new time cycle. Animals left to adjust at their own pace required 11 days or more to adapt.

People whose jobs require them to switch back and forth between day and night shifts often suffer from ulcers or other disorders. It appears to be less stressful to work at night and sleep in the daytime consistently than to change back and forth from one schedule to another. When it comes to sleep, it's healthy to be a "creature of habit."

Experiments involving the analysis of brain waves show that sleep involves four stages. As slumber progresses, brain-wave frequency decreases, but the amplitude (height) of the waves increases. An entire cycle (all four stages) takes about 90 minutes, and we normally pass through four or five cycles each night. People forced to sleep in the daytime rather than at night require about 3 weeks for the stages of their sleep cycle to return to normal.

Many human body cycles appear to follow a circadian rhythm. Urine production, for example, is usually at a minimum during sleep and reaches a peak during the morning hours. Excretion of sodium and potassium ions peaks around midday for most people, and hormonal secretions also follow a daily pattern. Body temperature, heart rate, and breathing rate change in predictable ways during the course of a day. Since these last three variables can be measured quite easily, you can conduct your own investigation of how they vary with time.

Investigation 2: Body Temperature, Heart Rate, Breathing Rate, and Time

To prevent any bias that might arise from self-examination, it's probably best to do this investigation with a partner. It will also provide twice as much data. At 2-hour intervals over as much of a 24-hour period as possible, measure your partner's body temperature, heart rate, and breathing rate. Your partner can make the same measurements on you.

Before you begin, have your partner sit down for 5 minutes. Then place a clean oral clinical thermometer under his or her tongue. Follow directions supplied with the thermometer concerning cleaning, shaking, and use. Be sure to sterilize the thermometer each time you use it. If there are no directions, ask a school nurse or another knowledgeable adult to help you.

While waiting for the thermometer to reach equilibrium, you can find your partner's heart rate and breathing rate. To determine the heart rate, take his or her pulse. Place your two middle fingers as shown in Figure 1 on the underside of your partner's wrist a short distance behind the point where the thumb joins the wrist. You should be able to feel a pulse, which is actually an expansion wave that travels along the arteries from the heart each time it contracts. Your fingers intercept the wave as it moves through the radial artery in the wrist. To find the heart rate in beats per minute, count the number of pulses you feel over a 30-second period and multiply that number by 2.

To determine your partner's breathing rate in breaths per minute, watch to see how many times his or her chest moves up and down in 1 minute. Or listen

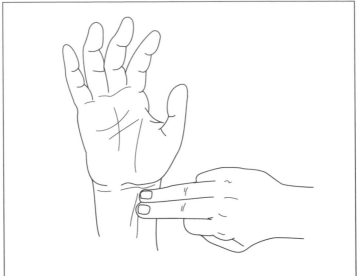

Figure 1. To take a person's pulse, place your two middle fingers on the underside of either wrist.

carefully and count the number of times he or she inhales and exhales in 1 minute. You'll notice that each inhalation is accompanied by a rising chest and each exhalation by a falling chest. After you've recorded your partner's temperature, heart rate, and breathing rate, he or she can make similar measurements on you.

How does your temperature change during the course of a day? Do your heart and breathing rates follow a similar pattern? Plot a graph of the temperatures and the rates versus time. Plot time on the horizontal axis and the other variables on the vertical axis. Use a different colored pencil or different symbol for each variable on the vertical axis, as shown in Figure 2. If possible, repeat your measurements over several days.

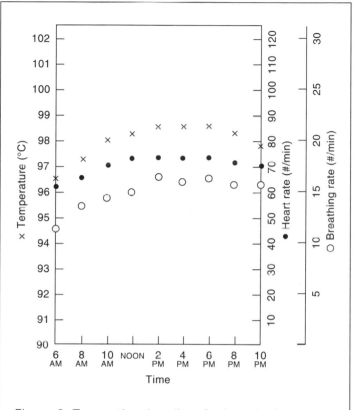

Figure 2. To see the circadian rhythms in the human body, graph a person's body temperature, heart rate, and breathing rate over a 16-hour period. How does this graph compare with yours?

How do your temperature, heart rate, and breathing rate vary with time? Do any of the patterns suggest a circadian rhythm? What do you notice about the ratio of heart rate to breathing rate?

Do your partner's temperature, heart rate, and

breathing rate show patterns similar to yours? How about his or her ratio of heart rate to breathing rate?

Investigation 3: Day People, Night People, and Punctual People

You may know someone who is regarded as a day person or a night person. Some people are slow to awaken but are very alert at night when others are ready to retire. Day people usually wake up "bright-eyed and bushy-tailed," ready and eager to take on life's challenges.

To see if you can distinguish "night owls" from day persons, try asking people these questions: "At what time of day do you feel you are most alert and do your best work?" "At what time do you go to bed?" "Do you need an alarm clock to awaken in the morning?" How can you identify night owls on the basis of these questions?

Can you classify people on the basis of punctuality? Are there people who are almost always on time for meetings and various events, and others who are invariably late? Are there "early birds" who usually arrive ahead of time? Can you devise a questionnaire that will allow you to identify these people?

BODY TEMPERATURE AND TIME

You may have heard that normal body temperature is 37.0°C, or 98.6°F. But *normal* is a deceptive word with regard to body temperature because your temperature changes over the course of a day. It is generally lower at night than in the daytime, when you are more active. This is because your internal temperature is related to your metabolic rate. A high metabolic rate is also related to your ability to handle mental tasks. People score significantly better on tests taken between 2 P.M. and 4 P.M. than they do on tests administered between 2 A.M. and 4 A.M. In the morning hours, your oxygen consumption and rate of metabolism are at a minimum.

Tests reveal people count faster when their body temperatures and metabolic rates are higher. The higher counting rate suggests that under these conditions internal subjective processes (internal clocks) appear to "tick" faster than external processes measured objectively with a clock. Such results have led some to suggest that children's higher metabolic rates explain why clock time seems to drag for youngsters but moves ever too swiftly for older people with characteristically lower metabolic rates. Others believe as discussed earlier that the ratio of present time to past time is the reason time passes so slowly for the young.

Project 2
Write an essay about a world without clocks. If all timekeeping instruments suddenly disappeared, how would it affect today's society? How would it have affected society in colonial America? In ancient Greece?

Investigation 4: Estimating Time
You might suspect that members of a time-conscious society would be very capable of estimating elapsed time. To see how well you do at this task, ask a friend or family member with a clock or watch to indicate a starting time by saying, "Begin!" Without counting in

any way or using a timepiece, try to estimate when 10 seconds have passed; when 30 seconds have passed; when an hour has transpired. How close were your estimates to the actual elapsed times?

Ask different people to try the same experiment. Are some people better at estimating time than others? Are adults better at this task than children? Do people in certain occupations seem to have a better knack for estimating elapsed time than others?

Repeat the experiment but this time allow people to use any vocal time-estimating methods they wish. For example, someone might say, "Mississippi one, Mississippi two, Mississippi three . . ." or "Twenty-one, twenty-two, twenty-three . . ." or another of the various methods used to measure seconds without a watch. Do people using any of these methods make better estimates of elapsed time than they did before?

Estimate the time required to do activities such as brushing your teeth, dressing, taking a bath or a shower, eating breakfast, or carrying out various other tasks. Then use a watch or clock to measure the time required for each activity. How do your estimated times compare with the actual times required to perform each of the activities?

Investigation 5: Measuring and Seeing Short Time Intervals

The phrase "quick as a wink!" implies that a wink or a blink of the eye takes but a short period of time. In this investigation you'll find out just how long it takes to blink, squeeze your hand, or type a word.

To measure the time it takes to blink, ask a friend

to use the second hand of a clock or watch to measure the time required for you to blink 30 times as fast as you can. How long did it take? Using the data you've collected, determine the time to blink once.

Ask other people to carry out the same experiment. Does it take everyone about the same time to blink?

Design experiments to find out how long it takes to squeeze a hand or type a word.

Cameras are equipped with a timing mechanism called a shutter to control the amount of light that reaches the film. To "see" short time intervals, open the back of an empty 35-mm camera that has an adjustable shutter speed. Set the shutter for 1/15 second. Then look into the back of the empty camera and push the shutter release button. You will see light coming through the front of the camera for 1/15 second. Repeat the experiment for shutter speeds of 1/30, 1/60, 1/100, 1/250, and 1/1000 second.

When you look through a camera with its shutter set for a speed of 1/1000 (0.001 or 10^{-3}) second, you are "seeing" a millisecond. Even smaller time intervals are used by physicists, who sometimes measure time in microseconds (10^{-6} s), nanoseconds (10^{-9} s), or picoseconds (10^{-12} s).

The images that form on your eye do not disappear immediately. They fade away after about 1/15 second. Consequently, the action seen in movies shown at a rate of 24 or 32 frames per second appears to be continuous rather than a series of still pictures.

To see this effect in a somewhat simpler setting, use crayons to draw a bright-colored fish on one side of a white file card. On the other side, draw a fish tank. Put

the card in the jaws of a spring-type clothespin and tape
the other end of the clothespin to the end of a wooden
dowel or pencil. If you now rotate the dowel rapidly
between your hands, you will see that the fish appears
to be in the tank.

Investigation 6: Time and Cameras

A camera's shutter speed determines how long the film
is exposed to light. To see the effect of exposure time
on film, you will need a camera in which the shutter
speed can be adjusted manually. Use the camera to take
a picture of the same still scene at different shutter
speeds. Be sure to record the shutter speed and the number of the frame for each picture you take.

After the film has been developed, compare the
photographs or the frames on a proof sheet. How does
the shutter speed affect the photograph?

Next, take photographs of moving objects at different shutter speeds. You might, for example, take photographs of children on a merry-go-round or cars passing your house or school at about the same speed. How
does the shutter speed affect the photograph? Can you
explain why?

Try taking some time exposures of moving lights,
such as car headlights at night as shown in the photograph on the opposite page. With your camera perfectly
still, open the shutter for about a minute while you photograph a light that is moving. One approach is to make
a lighted flashlight the bob of a pendulum by attaching
some rope or heavy string and letting the flashlight hang
down. Then get the light moving in elliptical paths
above your upward-pointed camera.

A shutter, the timing mechanism on a camera, lets
light in for only fractions of a second. If the shutter
is held open for about a minute, the result is a
photograph like this one of car headlights along
the Schuylkill Expressway in Philadelphia.

Project 3

*Take time exposures of landscapes illuminated by
moonlight. Here, you will probably need exposures
of several minutes or more.*

On a night when there is no moonlight, take

some time-lapse photographs of the stars. Clamp your camera to a tripod, post, or railing and point it toward the North Star. Try exposures of a few minutes to several hours. What do your photographs reveal? Does it make a difference whether you use color or black-and-white film? Why might stars have different colors?

TIME AND ANIMALS

The annual migrations of birds, whales, and other animals indicate that they possess internal clocks. What is it that stimulates them to travel across lines of latitude? Is it changes in temperature? The ratio of hours of light to hours of darkness? Changes in the Sun's path across the sky? We know that animals are sensitive to both light and temperature. A total eclipse of the Sun, for example, will cause crickets to chirp and chickens and other birds to roost as they do at night.

In winter, the fur of snowshoe rabbits turns white, a camouflage that protects them from predators in snow. Experiments have shown that lowering the temperature does not change the fur color. However, a gradual reduction in the number of hours of sunlight, even when the environment was maintained at summer temperatures, was accompanied by the growth of the white winter coat.

Karl von Frisch, an Austrian zoologist who early in this century studied the way honey bees communicate, also investigated their internal clock. He found that if fed sugar at a certain time of day, bees would soon learn to be at the feeding place at the same time

Snowshoe rabbits are cam-
ouflaged in the snow during
wintertime, when their fur
is white. In the spring, their
internal clocks cause their
fur to turn brown, as shown
in the photo to the right. Are
their clocks based on outdoor temperature or the
amount of daylight?

every day. Von Frisch prepared two identical rooms, one in Paris and one in New York, five time zones west of Paris. When the bees were flown from Paris to New York, he found that they continued to look for their food according to Paris time. If they had been feeding at 10 A.M. in Paris, they went to their normal feeding place at 5 A.M. New York time.

Investigation 7: Are Pets Attuned to Circadian Rhythms?

If you own a pet, watch its behavior. Does it show evidence of 24-hour behavior cycles? For instance, does it sleep during certain hours of the day? Does it look for food at the time it's normally fed? Or is it simply responding to your actions when you prepare the food? Try delaying your pet's feeding time. How does it respond? Does it go to its feeding dish and look for food? Does it engage in behavior that suggests it's trying to remind you that it's time to eat?

You can probably observe your pet's breathing rate, and you may be able to feel its heart beating if you place your hand on its chest. Does your pet's breathing rate show a circadian rhythm? How about its heart rate?

The Panamanian three-hour bird, a small ostrich-like animal that sings every 3 hours, has a more precise internal clock than most animals. But few have a long-term sense of time that can compare with that of the swallows who return to San Juan Capistrano, California, on March 19 each year. If we look to the sea, we find animals with internal clocks set to the tides. At approximately 2-week intervals (near new and full moons) when high tides are at their peak levels, small fish called grunions can be found laying their eggs along beaches. Two weeks later, at the next peak high tide, the eggs hatch and the baby grunions are captured by the ocean.

Fiddler crabs also have a "clock" tied to the ocean's tides, as well as to light. During daylight hours, the crabs are dark greenish brown in color; at night, they turn a pale brown. Their daylight color, however, is darkest at low tide, which occurs about 50 minutes later each day. The darker color provides better camouflage as the crabs feed on the green algae left on the dark mud that remains when the ocean recedes.

You might expect oysters to have a clock set to the tides and, indeed they do. Oysters harvested from the shores of Long Island Sound in New Haven, Connecticut, were transported to Illinois, 1,300 km (800 mi) inland, in containers filled with seawater. In terms of sun-time, Illinois is about an hour west of Connecticut. The oysters, who opened their shells widest at high tide, continued to do so at a time corresponding to high tide in New Haven. Two weeks later, they had adjusted to their new location and were opening their shells widest about an hour later, at the time high tide would occur if Illinois were on the ocean.

Of the animals that hibernate during the winter, such as woodchucks, ground squirrels, and bats, none is more fascinating than *Ursus americanus*, the black bear. No one knows for certain what triggers a bear's internal clock and causes it to lie down for a long winter nap. Nor do we know why in late summer, bears begin to spend as much as 20 hours each day eating almost everything they can find. By the time they go into hibernation, adult bears may have a layer of fat 12 cm (5 in) thick.

The body temperature of many hibernators, such as ground squirrels, falls from 98°F (37°C) to 34°F (1°C) and their heart rates slow from 350 beats per minute to 4 or 5 beats per minute. A black bear's metabolic rate does not show such a phenomenal decrease. Its heart rate falls from 40 beats per minute to about 8 beats per minute, but its body temperature drops only about 9 degrees below its normal 100°F.

During their 4 months of hibernation, bears do not eat or drink, do not urinate or defecate. Some water is lost through the bear's lungs and skin, but its body replenishes it by "burning" fat, a metabolizing process that produces water and carbon dioxide. Because bears metabolize very little protein during hibernation, they produce only a small amount of the urea that results from the process. Normally, urea is excreted from the body in urine, but the small amount produced during hibernation is broken down and recycled to form new protein.

Because of their ability to shut down urine production and recycle urea, bears are of great interest to medical researchers as well as naturalists. Many researchers believe that the secret to treating kidney failure in humans lies in the physiology of hibernating bears. Humans can live only a few days if their kidneys cease filtering urea and other toxic substances from their blood. Today people whose kidneys fail must either have a kidney transplantation or undergo periodic hemodialysis, in which a machine filters their blood.

No one knows for certain what triggers a bear's internal clock and causes the animal to hibernate for four months every winter.

Researchers hope that some way may be found to shut down urine production and to recycle urea in humans in the same way as in bears.

Investigation 8: Crickets and Temperature
Crickets are sensitive to temperature and light. Generally, you hear the chirping of crickets after dark. As

autumn approaches and evening temperatures drop, you'll find the crickets' chirping rate falls too. Some people claim you can use a cricket as a thermometer. They say that if you count the number of chirps a cricket makes in 14 seconds and add 40, you will have the Fahrenheit temperature within two degrees.

Test this claim by counting a cricket's chirps on a variety of days when the temperature is noticeably different. Can a cricket and a watch serve as a thermometer?

Project 4
Watch several species of birds common to your area in the summer. Do they begin migrating during the first cold snap, or do they remain despite cool temperatures until the days grow shorter? Do different species respond to different signals?

THE
EARLY HISTORY
OF
KEEPING TIME

Early humans had no need for small units of time. Their day began with sunrise and ended with sunset. They knew that when the Sun reached its highest point in the sky, the day was half over, and many of them stopped working to eat and rest. They had no need for hours, minutes, or seconds. There were no train or airplane schedules to meet, no school bus arriving at 8:03, and no movies starting at 6:45. Most people traveled no farther than the edge of their village because walking was their only means of travel.

Throughout history, humans have watched the seasons change with time. They learned to plant seeds in the spring, harvest their crops in the summer and autumn, and store food for the cool or cold days of winter. Calendars were invented to keep track of passing days. Calendars enabled people to celebrate religious holidays at the proper time, to anticipate the change of seasons and rainy periods or floods, and to prepare for

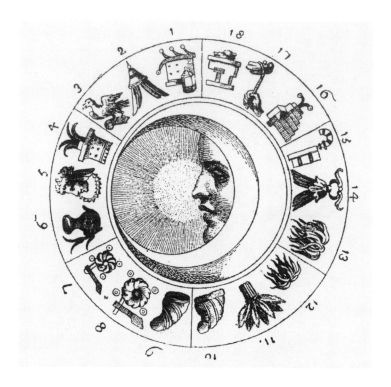

This Aztec calendar was designed to keep track of the changing seasons.

the arrival of migrating herds of mammals, flocks of birds, or schools of fish, all of which were a source of food. But it was a long time before they developed accurate calendars and could explain what caused seasons to change with time.

Investigation 9: Time and Seasons, A Global View

To see why we have a change in seasons on Earth, you can make a model of the Earth's orbit around the Sun. A bright, frosted light bulb in an otherwise dark room can represent the Sun. A large, white polystyrene plastic (Styrofoam) ball, such as the kind used in Christmas decorations, can represent the Earth. Stick a toothpick into the top of the ball. It will represent the Earth's North Pole. A second toothpick can be used both to represent the South Pole and to serve as a handle.

Hold the "Earth" several feet from the "Sun" as shown in Figure 3a. You should see a shadow on the side of the Earth away from the Sun. No sunlight enters this shadow, which extends from the North Pole to the South Pole. Rotate the Earth around its axis (the imaginary line connecting its poles) and watch different areas of its surface enter and leave the shadow. What period of time is represented by one rotation?

If the Earth's axis were perpendicular to a line connecting the Earth to the Sun, as it is now in your model, there would no seasonal changes. However, the Earth's axis is actually tilted at an angle of 23.5° as shown in Figure 3b. In your Earth-Sun model, tilt the Earth's axis by roughly this amount. What happens to the regions of the Earth that are in shadow and light?

Keeping the axis of the Earth tilted, move it around the "Sun" as shown in Figure 3c. Notice what happens to the regions of the Earth covered by shadow. If you live in the Northern Hemisphere, which position of the Earth in Figure 3c do you think represents the Earth at the beginning of summer in the Northern Hemisphere (approximately June 20)? At the beginning of winter (approximately December 20)? Which positions represent the Earth at the beginning of spring? At the beginning of fall? Explain the reasoning you used in answering each question.

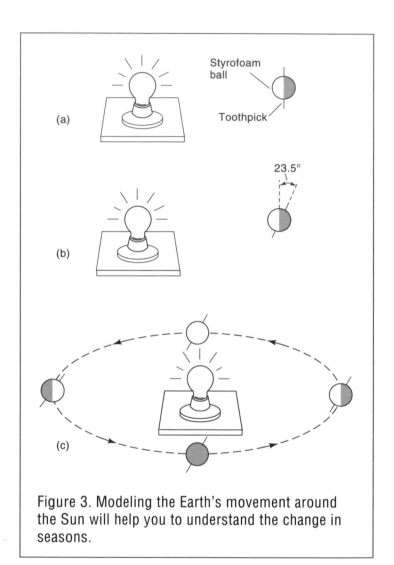

Figure 3. Modeling the Earth's movement around the Sun will help you to understand the change in seasons.

At the position representing summer, slowly rotate the Earth around its axis. Which part of the Earth remains in light throughout the entire rotation? Which part remains in darkness?

Can you tell from your model how the number of hours of daylight and darkness depends on the season? If not, have a friend hold the ball tilted so that the Sun shines on the North Pole as it did when the ball was on the left side of the diagram in Figure 3c. Which season is this in the Northern Hemisphere?

Use a marking pen to place a dot on the edge of the shadow in the middle of the Northern Hemisphere and another dot in the middle of the Southern Hemisphere as shown in Figure 4. While you watch the dots, ask your friend to rotate the Earth slowly so that the dots pass through "sunrise," "noon," and "afternoon." When the dot in the Southern Hemisphere reenters the Earth's shadow at "sunset," where is the dot in the Northern Hemisphere?

Repeat the experiment with the Earth tilted to the Sun as it was on the right of Figure 3c. Which season is this in the Northern Hemisphere? Now which hemisphere has more hours of daylight?

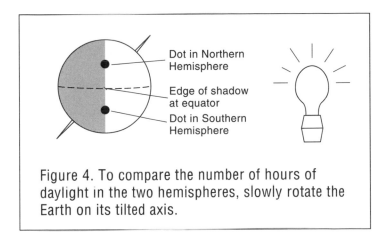

Dot in Northern Hemisphere

Edge of shadow at equator

Dot in Southern Hemisphere

Figure 4. To compare the number of hours of daylight in the two hemispheres, slowly rotate the Earth on its tilted axis.

THE CHANGING MOON—ANOTHER UNIT OF TIME

The first unit of time was the day—the time from one sunrise or one midday to the next. But the ever-changing moon revealed another uniform pattern of time that marked a longer interval.

Investigation 10: Watching and Timing the Moon

Most people have seen a full moon during the evening or at dawn, but many do not know that the moon is often visible during daylight hours. If you look for and watch the moon over a period of several months, you'll learn much about this celestial body and the time unit related to it.

You'll need a notebook to record the moon's locations and changes in appearance over the next few months. Try to observe where and when the moon rises every day, or as often as you can see it. It's probably easiest to start with a full moon, which rises at about the same time that the Sun sets. How does the moon's appearance change from one day or week to the next? How do its rising and setting times change over the same periods?

About how much time elapses between the new moon, when the moon can't be seen, and the first quarter, when the moon is half-lighted (a quarter of the moon's complete cycle)? Between first quarter and full moon? Between full moon and third quarter, when the moon is half-lighted, but on the side opposite the one that was lighted at first quarter? Between third quarter and new moon? How many days pass between one full moon and the next? From your observations and records, what unit of time is most closely related to the moon's full cycle?

Investigation 11: A Model of the Moon's Cycle

Use the same light bulb you used to represent the Sun in Investigation 9. A large white polystyrene plastic (Styrofoam) ball can serve as the moon. Your own head can represent the Earth. Stand some distance from the bulb in an otherwise dark room and hold the ball (moon) at arm's length as in Figure 5. Turn very slowly so that the ball moves around you in a circle representing the moon's orbit around the Earth. Since your head represents the Earth, the moon, as you see it in this model, is the way it is seen on Earth.

Where must the moon be with respect to the Earth

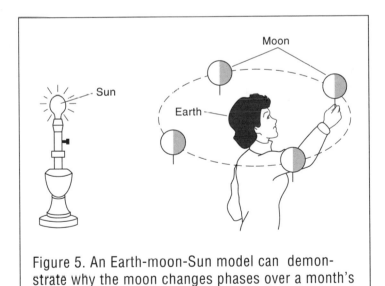

Figure 5. An Earth-moon-Sun model can demonstrate why the moon changes phases over a month's time.

and Sun to be seen as a full moon? As a new moon? A crescent moon that sets soon after the Sun? A moon at first quarter? A moon at last quarter? A crescent moon that rises slightly before the Sun? How would the Earth look at each of these times as seen from the moon?

How could you use your model to show an eclipse of the moon? An eclipse of the Sun?

A MOON-BASED CALENDAR

More than 3,000 years before Christ, the Babylonians, who were fortunate enough to have clear night skies, established a 12-month calendar based on the moon's cycle. They found that between one full moon and the next, the Sun rose 29 times in one cycle and 30 times in the next. This led them to conclude that the moon's period (the time to orbit the Earth once) was 29.5 days. How does this compare with your estimate of the moon's period?

It didn't make much sense to change months at half-day intervals so their months alternated between 29 and 30 days. However, the total number of days in six 29-day months and six 30-day months is only 354. The Babylonians soon realized that their year was about 11 days too short, so they added a few days periodically to make up the deficiency.

THE EGYPTIANS AND A BETTER CALENDAR

The Egyptians were good astronomers. They discovered that while the positions of most stars remained unchanged, there were a few "stars" that seemed to move slowly across the sky relative to the others. We now know that those wandering stars were the planets that, like Earth, revolve around the Sun. The Egyptians wisely used the distant stars, not the wanderers, to establish their year and calendar. The stars were in essence a celestial clock.

Although the distant stars do not move with respect to each other, they all appear to move across the sky with the Sun throughout the day because of the Earth's rotation. They also shift slowly with respect to the Sun throughout the year as the Earth revolves around the Sun. The brightest star in the sky is Sirius, which is in the constellation Canis Major shown in Figure 6. Egyptian priests marked the beginning of their year as the day that Sirius rose with the Sun. A tunnel in one of the pyramids was oriented toward the point at which Sirius rose above the horizon. The day that this happened was important because it was soon followed

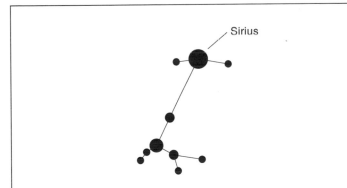

Figure 6. Egyptians set the beginning of their year as the day Sirius, the brightest star in the sky, rises with the Sun. Sirius is in the constellation Canis Major, which is Latin for "big dog."

This photograph shows that the star Sirius is far brighter than the other stars in the sky.

by the flooding of the Nile, an event that brought fresh soil to the farmland.

The Egyptian calendar consisted of twelve 30-day months. But this calendar year did not end with a new sighting of Sirius rising with the Sun because it was about 5 days short of a full year. As a result, they had to add 5 or 6 "monthless" days to each year.

After hundreds of years, the priests noticed that Sirius was no longer rising at exactly the same point. Centuries later, its rising could no longer even be viewed through the tunnel. The Egyptians could not explain why this had happened. Today, we know that their observations were the first evidence that the Earth's axis is precessing like a top as shown in Figure 7.

As a result of the precession, in which a full cycle takes nearly 26,000 years, the stars appear to shift incrementally relative to the Earth every year. For example, the North Star, also known as Polaris, will slowly move away from its position above the Earth's North Pole over the next few millennia. In about 12,000 years, the bright star Vega in the constellation Lyra will be closely aligned with the North Pole.

ROME AND THE JULIAN CALENDAR

The earliest Roman calendar evolved without help from astronomers. That explains why it was so out of alignment with natural events: a year contained only the 10 months shown in Table 1.

TABLE 1: The Ten Months of a Roman Calendar	
Name of Month	Number of Days
Martius	31
Aprilis	30
Maius	31
Junius	30
Quintilus	31
Sextilis	30
September	30
October	31
November	30
December	30

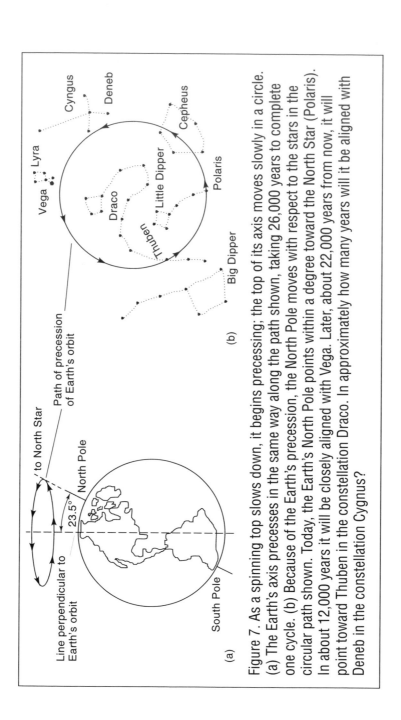

Figure 7. As a spinning top slows down, it begins precessing; the top of its axis moves slowly in a circle. (a) The Earth's axis precesses in the same way along the path shown, taking 26,000 years to complete one cycle. (b) Because of the Earth's precession, the North Pole moves with respect to the stars in the circular path shown. Today, the Earth's North Pole points within a degree toward the North Star (Polaris). In about 12,000 years it will be closely aligned with Vega. Later, about 22,000 years from now, it will point toward Thuben in the constellation Draco. In approximately how many years will it be aligned with Deneb in the constellation Cygnus?

If you count the total number of days, you will find that the first Roman calendar has only 304. The priests, who had some knowledge of astronomy, knew there was a problem but had no power to change the calendar. Consequently, after the last day of December, everyone would patiently wait for the priests to announce the beginning of a new year on Martius 1.

Project 5

In Latin, decem *means ten, and December was originally the tenth month. We see parts of this Latin word in* decade, *which means 10 years, and in* decimal, *which designates tenths. What other months in the old Roman calendar were associated with a number? What was the source of the names of the other months?*

In about 700 B.C., King Numa Pompilius changed the calendar. He added two months—Januarius and Februarius—between December and Martius. To take lunar time into account, the months alternated between 29 and 30 days so that each could begin with a new moon. Numa's calendar was an improvement, but it was still about 11 days shy of a year. To compensate, an additional short month called Mercedinus consisting alternately of 22 and 23 days was added to the calendar every 2 years.

By 46 B.C., so many rulers had adjusted the calendar for their own political purposes that the first day of spring was arriving 3 months late. The first day of spring should coincide with the vernal equinox, when the Sun crosses the equator as it moves northward.

Because of the discrepancy, Julius Caesar hired the Alexandrian astronomer Sosigenes to help him devise a better calendar for the Roman Empire. The Julian calendar they developed had the following features:

- A year consisted of 365 days with 12 months of 30 or 31 days each, except for February, which had 29 days.
- Because Sosigenes knew that it took $365\frac{1}{4}$ days, not 365, for the Sun to make a full cycle to the south and north across the sky, the Julian calendar added 1 day to the month of February every fourth year. Today we call that year a leap year. This made the average year $365\frac{1}{4}$ days in length.
- To move the vernal equinox back to the month of March, Caesar added 3 months—80 days to be precise—to the year 46 B.C. That year became known as the "year of confusion." The Julian calendar took effect after this long year on January 1, 45 B.C. (Of course, it wasn't known as a B.C. year at that time.)
- The Romans believed that uneven numbers were lucky, so they assigned 31 days to the odd-numbered months —Januarius, Martius, Maius, Quintilus, September, and November—and 30 days to the even-numbered months—Aprilis, Junius, Sextilis, October, and December. February, the only exception, was given 29 days, except in leap years, when it had 30 days.

After Julius Caesar's death, Quintilus, the fifth month in the old Roman calendar, was renamed July in his honor. Later, Sextilis, originally the sixth month, was renamed to honor Julius's successor, Augustus Caesar. At the same time, August was given a lucky 31 days at the expense of February, which was reduced to 28 days.

THE GREGORIAN CALENDAR

The Julian calendar worked well for 1500 years, until time caught up with it again. A year is actually 11 minutes and 14 seconds shorter than $365^1/4$ days. By 1582, 1,627 years after the Julian calendar was adopted, this small difference in time was causing the vernal equinox to occur in early March instead of late March.

Project 6

Show that the time difference between the Julian year and the actual year adds up to a difference of nearly 13 days over the period from 45 B.C. to A.D. 1582.

The timing of the vernal equinox was important because Easter was traditionally celebrated on the first Sunday after the first full moon after the vernal equinox. The inaccuracy in the calendar meant that Easter was now occurring in March instead of April. To correct the problem, Pope Gregory XIII decreed that the day following October 4, 1582, would be October 15, not October 5.

Project 7

Show how Pope Gregory, by cutting ten days from October 1582, was able to move the vernal equinox from March 11 to March 21 in the following year.

To prevent the problem from occurring again, Pope Gregory established a new rule for leap years. Instead of having every year divisible by 4 be a leap year—as Caesar had decreed—the new rule established that century years shall be leap years only if they are divisible by 400. As a result, the years 1700, 1800, and 1900 were not leap years, but the year 2000 will be. This Gregorian calendar is the one we use today.

Project 8

Will the Gregorian calendar's rule about leap year completely eliminate the need to add or subtract days from the calendar in the years ahead? If not, how often will days have to be added or dropped from the year? What other method might be used to prevent the need to change the calendar again?

Catholic countries put the Gregorian calendar into effect in 1582, but Protestant countries such as England and those under the control of the Eastern Church delayed acceptance until much later. During this time of calendar differences, the dates of events that took place in England and the colonies were often followed by the words "old style" to distinguish them from the dates on the Gregorian calendar. One example is the plaque in front of Town Hall in Eastham, Massachusetts, shown in the photograph on p. 55.

It was not until 1752 that Great Britain and the American colonies made the conversion to the Gregorian calendar. By decree of Britain's Parliament, September 2, 1752, was followed by September 14. However, more

ONE MILE WEST OF THIS SITE
HOSTILE INDIANS HAD THEIR

FIRST ENCOUNTER

6 DECEMBER 1620
(OLD STYLE)

WITH MYLES STANDISH, JOHN CARVER,
WILLIAM BRADFORD, EDWARD WINSLOW,
JOHN TILLEY, EDWARD TILLEY, JOHN
HOWLAND, RICHARD WARREN, STEPHEN
HOPKINS, EDWARD DOTEY, JOHN ALLERTON,
THOMAS ENGLISH, MASTER MATE CLARK,
MASTER GUNNER COPIN AND THREE
SAILORS OF THE MAYFLOWER COMPANY

THIS TABLET IS PLACED IN 1920 BY THE
SOCIETY OF COLONIAL WARS IN THE
COMMONWEALTH OF MASSACHUSETTS

The phrase "old style" underneath the date on this plaque in front of Town Hall in Eastham, Massachusetts, indicates the date is based on the Julian calendar, rather than our modern Gregorian calendar.

than another century passed before some countries, including Japan and China, adopted the Gregorian calendar. Russia did not adopt the "new style" calendar until 1918.

CALENDAR REFORM

While the Gregorian calendar has become a part of our culture, there are two major movements to reform it. Among the reasons for reforming the Gregorian calendar are the following:

- The months vary in length from 28 to 31 days.
- No date falls on the same day of the week in two consecutive years. For example, if the Fourth of July falls on Monday one year, it will fall on Tuesday the next year—or on Wednesday if the next year is a leap year.
- A year or a month may begin on any day of the week. As a result, the number of weekdays varies from month to month.
- It is difficult to determine on what day of the week any given holiday will fall in future years.
- The lack of consistency in the calendar creates practical problems for certain people. People who are paid on a monthly basis have a fixed amount of money to pay bills for utilities and other daily services. But these charges vary according to the number of days in the month. People paid every other week may receive 27 paychecks in one year and 26 in another.

Can you find other disadvantages or problems in the Gregorian calendar?

There are two major calendar reform movements. One advocates a 13-month calendar, in which each month has 28 days. Each month would begin on a Sunday and end on a Sunday. However, since $13 \times 28 = 364$, a year-end holiday or extra Saturday would be added to each year. On leap years, there would be an additional holiday that could fall at the end of the year or at the end of any chosen month.

The other reform movement calls for what is known as a world calendar. Less radical than the 13-month calendar, it would still contain 12 months, but their lengths would change to make every quarter of the year identical. The months of January, February, and March would be identical with the second-quarter months of April, May, and June; the third-quarter months of July, August, and September; and the fourth-quarter months of October, November, and December. The first month in each quarter would have 31 days and begin on a Sunday. The second and third months in each quarter would have 30 days, and the third month would end on a Saturday.

Following Saturday, December 30, there would be a holiday called Worldsday—an extra Saturday preceding Sunday, January 1, of the following year. On leap years, there would be a second Worldsday following June 30.

Project 9

Use pencil, paper, and a ruler to draw the proposed 13-month calendar and the world calendar. What problems in the present calendar would be solved by the 13-month calendar? By the world calendar? Can you see any problems that might be created by either of these proposed calendars?

Develop and draw a reform calendar of your own. What are the advantages of your calendar over the present calendar? Over the world calendar and the 13-month calendar?

THE WEEK—A HUMAN INVENTION

A day, a month, and a year are, or were, based on natural intervals—one rotation of the Earth, one revolution of the moon about the Earth, and one revolution of the Earth about the Sun. A 7-day week, on the other hand, has no natural basis; it is a human invention based on a social convention developed in the distant past. In fact, history reveals that weeks with more or less than 7 days have existed. Each month of the 12-month Egyptian year contained three 10-day weeks. The start of each week was marked by the rising of a main star in one of the 36 constellations that made up the Egyptian celestial clock.

One source of the 7-day week is the Jewish religion. According to the book of Genesis, "So God blessed the seventh day and hallowed it, because on it God rested from all his work which he had done in creation." Another possible source is the astrology of the Chaldeans who ruled ancient Babylonia. They knew of the seven wanderers (the five planets, the Sun, and the moon) and believed that they influenced human fortunes. Had they known of the planets Uranus, Neptune, and Pluto, which were discovered between 1781 and 1930, we would probably have a 10-day week.

The Chaldeans believed that each day was influenced by a different wanderer. Originally, the Romans named each day of the week for the Sun, the moon, or the planet in their Latin language. But with time, some

TABLE 2: The Origin of the Days of the Week		
Day	**Wanderer**	**Origin of Name**
Sunday	Sun	*dies solis* (Sun's day)
Monday	Moon	*dies lunae* (moon's day)
Tuesday	Mars	Originally *dies Martis* (Mars's day); then *Tiw's day*, for Tiw, a god of battle associated with Mars, the god of war
Wednesday	Mercury	Originally *dies mercurii* (Mercury's day); then *Woden's day* for Woden, a god of battle associated with mercury because of his wisdom and magic
Thursday	Jupiter	Originally *dies Jovis* (Jupiter's day—Jove was another name for Jupiter); then *Thor's day* for Thor, god of thunder
Friday	Venus	Originally *dies Veneris* (Venus's day), then *Frigg's day* for Frigg, the wife of Woden, who like Venus, was a goddess of fertility and love
Saturday	Saturn	*dies Saturni* (Saturn's day)

of the days came to be named for Germanic deities who, in one way or another, were associated with the original planet for that day. (See Table 2.)

How the days of the week came to be ordered the way they are is a matter of speculation, too. If the order were based on increasing distance of the wanderer from the Earth, the days would run Monday, Friday, Tuesday, Wednesday, Sunday, Thursday, and Saturday. The order of the wanderers in terms of their periods—the time it takes to complete one cycle in the sky with respect to the Earth—is moon, Mercury, Venus, Sun, Mars, Jupiter, Saturn. Thus, period cannot account for the way the days of the week are ordered either.

One way to produce the proper order of days is to arrange the planets by period starting with the longest cycle (Saturn) and then make leaps of two planets at a time. A schematic of such leaps, starting with Saturn, is shown in Figure 8a. Unfortunately, no one can offer any reasonable explanation for taking such an approach in ordering the days.

There is evidence that the Babylonians believed each hour of the day was watched over by one of the wanderers. Starting with Saturn and following the order of decreasing period, successive hours would be assigned as shown under Day 1 in Figure 8b. Assuming the major wanderer controlling the day was the planet of the first hour, you can see that by extending the hours and days, the controlling planet for successive days would be Saturn, Sun, moon, Mars, Mercury, Jupiter, Venus. This agrees nicely with the planetary leaps described earlier and assumes that hours of the day were established before days of the week.

We know that the Egyptians, whose culture coincided with that of the Babylonians, divided the day into 24 hours. There were 12 hours for night, 10 for day, and 1 hour each for dawn and dusk. These hours, however, were not of equal or constant length. During the summer, daylight hours were longer than night hours and longer than the daylight hours of winter.

Early Romans had a 9-day week consisting of 8

Hour	Day 1 wanderer	Hour	Day 2 wanderer	Hour	Day 3 wanderer
1	Saturn	1	Sun	1	Moon
2	Jupiter	2	Venus	2	⋮ ⋮
3	Mars	3	Mercury		
4	Sun	4	Moon		
5	Venus	5	Saturn		
6	Mercury	6	Jupiter		
7	Moon	7	Mars		
8	Saturn	8	Sun		
9	Jupiter	9	⋮ ⋮		
10	Mars				
11	Sun				
12	Venus				
13	Mercury				
14	Moon				
15	Saturn				
16	Jupiter				
17	Mars				
18	Sun				
19	Venus				
20	Mercury				
21	Moon				
22	Saturn	23	Venus		
23	Jupiter	24	Mercury		
24	Mars				

(b) Another way is to assume a wanderer rules each hour of the day and to name the day according to the ruler of the first hour.

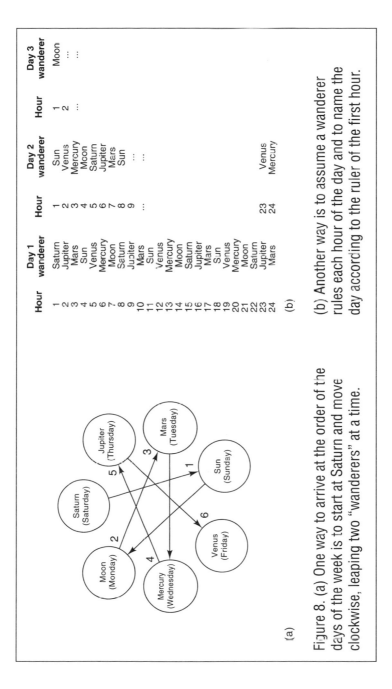

(a)

Figure 8. (a) One way to arrive at the order of the days of the week is to start at Saturn and move clockwise, leaping two "wanderers" at a time.

market days followed by one day of rest. But we know that they had adopted a 7-day week by A.D. 79, in the early days of Christianity. The first Christians were Jews, who at the time celebrated both the Sabbath (Saturday) and Sunday. The Christian church eventually took Sunday as its day of rest and worship because church fathers held that Christ, who was crucified on a Friday, ascended into Heaven on the following Sunday. In the fourth century A.D., the Church of Rome made Sunday the official day of worship.

There have been several attempts to change the seven-day week. In 1793, France, in its effort to decimalize all measurements and to separate church and state, installed a 10-day week. Each day contained 10 hours, each hour 100 minutes, and each minute 100 seconds. French churchgoers, however, persisted in worshiping and resting every seventh day. By 1805, Napoleon Bonaparte, as part of his reconciliation with the church, reinstated the Gregorian calendar and returned to the 24-hour day, the 60-minute hour, and the 60-second minute.

In 1929, the Soviet Union eliminated Saturday and Sunday from the week to help stamp out religion, which its Communist leaders regarded as the "opiate of the masses." They replaced the 5-day week with a 6-day week in 1931, but Russian peasants clung to the traditional week. Both religious pressure and the Gregorian calendar used by the rest of the world led them to return to the 7-day week in 1948. Although there are still a few places in Africa that use 10-day market cycles, most of the world now uses the 7-day week and the Gregorian calendar.

HEAVENLY TIME

For thousands of years astronomers have been our time-keepers. It was they, often serving as priests, who found in the stars ways to mark the beginning of a new year and the changes of season. And it was they who devised ways to divide the day into smaller units of time. You've seen how Egyptian astronomers used the bright star Sirius to mark the beginning of a new year, how the present 12-month calendar evolved, and how the 7-day week may have arisen. In this chapter, you'll learn how the Sun and stars are used to measure time. You'll learn, too, how the railroads devised ways to reduce the confusion that arose when time, as measured by the Sun, came into conflict with a growing technology that changed our concept of time and distance.

THE EARTH AND THE CELESTIAL SPHERE

The Earth is very nearly a sphere. If you started at the North Pole and moved due south to the South Pole, crossed the pole, and then continued north back to the North Pole, you would follow a circular path. Similarly, if you started at the equator and moved due east or west, you would return to your starting place, having followed the 40,000-kilometer (25,000-mile) path around the Earth's equator. As with any circle, these circles along the Earth's surface can be divided into degrees as shown in Figure 9. The imaginary lines parallel to the equator are called lines of latitude, and the equatorial circle is defined as 0°. Lines of longitude, or meridians, run from North Pole to South Pole. These longitude lines are great circles; that is, their centers are located at the center of the Earth. Which latitudinal circle is a great circle?

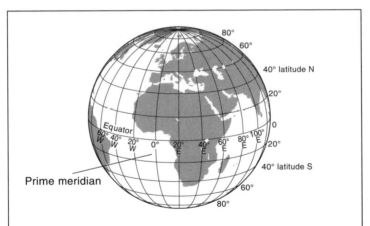

Figure 9. Lines of latitude circle the Earth parallel to the equator. Lines of longitude run from the North Pole to the South Pole. The prime meridian, which runs through Greenwich, England, is defined as 0°. From there, lines of longitude are designated up to 180° east and up to 180 ° west.

The longitudinal line through Greenwich, England, is called the *prime meridian*. By agreement, it is designated 0°; other longitudes are defined as degrees east or west of the prime meridian. Because there are 360° along each line of latitude and 24 hours in a day, the Sun will move 360°/24 hour = 15° per hour. Thus, every 15° of longitude constitutes an hour of time. Keeping in mind that the Sun moves from east to west, can you figure out what time it is in Philadelphia, at 75° west longitude, when it is noon in Greenwich, England?

Project 10

What is the approximate distance between lines of longitude 15° apart at: (1) the equator; (2) 45° latitude; (3) the North and South poles?

Astronomers call the domelike sky that surrounds the Earth the celestial sphere. We observe the movement of stars, planets, the moon, and the Sun along a celestial hemisphere. The two celestial hemispheres together can be thought of as a huge sphere concentric with the Earth; in other words, the sphere has the same center as the Earth. The north and south celestial poles lie above the Earth's poles as shown in Figure 10. The celestial equator lies above the Earth's equator. The meridians that bisect the Earth's surface from pole to pole extend to the celestial sphere.

As you learned in Investigation 9, the Earth's axis is tilted 23.5° relative to its orbit around the Sun. From the Earth's frame of reference (the way things look to us), the Sun appears to move along an annual path

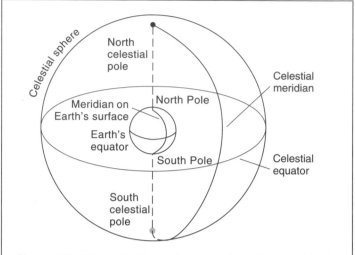

Figure 10. The celestial sphere, an imaginary object representing the sky, has poles, equator, and meridians that are extensions of the Earth's poles, equator, and meridians.

called the ecliptic, shown in Figure 11. The ecliptic is at an angle of 23.5° to the celestial equator—and to the Earth's equator. At the summer solstice, about June 20 in the Northern Hemisphere, the Sun is at its highest point on the ecliptic in Figure 11. At the winter solstice, about December 20, the Sun's path reaches its lowest point on the ecliptic. The vernal equinox, which marks the beginning of spring, occurs when the Sun crosses the celestial equator on its gradual northward movement along the ecliptic. The autumnal equinox, which marks the start of autumn around September 20, occurs when the Sun again crosses the celestial equator on a path carrying it southward.

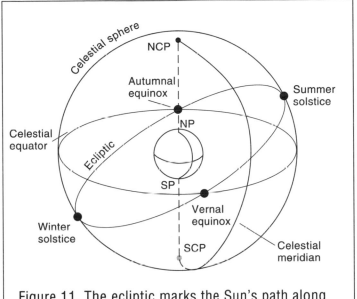

Figure 11. The ecliptic marks the Sun's path along the celestial sphere.

Investigation 12: Mapping the Sun's Path on the Celestial Sphere

To see how the Sun's path across the sky changes with time, you can map its path along the celestial sphere in at least two ways. One way is to use a clear plastic dome or a large, fine-mesh cooking strainer to represent the celestial hemisphere. You can find clear domes, or hemispheres, in a hobby store, your school, or a science supply house catalog. Place the dome or strainer on a sheet of heavy cardboard, and with a pencil or pen, draw the outline of its circular base on the cardboard. Remove the hemisphere and mark a dot at the very center of the circle you drew. The dot represents you at the center of the celestial hemisphere. Replace the dome or hemisphere and tape it securely to the cardboard.

Tape the cardboard with the hemisphere to a level surface in an open outdoor space shortly after sunrise. If you are using a clear dome, place the tip of a marking pen on the dome so that its shadow falls as shown in Figure 12a on the dot you marked at the center of the hemisphere. Mark this point on the dome. Why does the mark on the dome represent the Sun's position on the celestial hemisphere?

If you use a strainer, you can mark the Sun's position with round-headed pins stuck through the mesh or small pieces of masking tape stuck to the mesh as in Figure 12b.

Continue to mark the Sun's position at one-hour or half-hour intervals throughout the day. At the end of the day you will have a map of the Sun's path across the sky. How would you describe this path?

Repeat the experiment on different days during a 1-year period. If possible, try to map the Sun's path at times close to the vernal and autumnal equinoxes and the summer and winter solstices.

For each map you have made, look at Figure 11 and consider the Sun's position on the ecliptic on that day. Can you explain how the Sun's position on the ecliptic, coupled with the Earth's turning, led to each of the maps you have drawn?

THE SUN'S PATH AND YOUR POSITION ON EARTH

The Sun's path across the sky depends on where you live. At the North Pole, Polaris is almost directly overhead, and the plane on which you stand is parallel to the

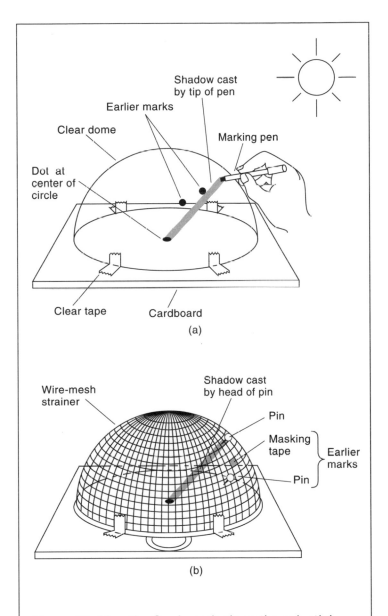

Figure 12. Map the Sun's path along the celestial hemisphere using (a) a clear plastic dome or (b) a wire mesh strainer.

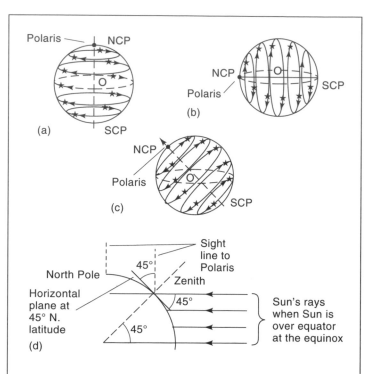

Figure 13. The way the stars move across the celestial sphere depends upon the latitude of an observer on Earth. (a) An observer 0 at the North Pole sees the stars moving in circles parallel to the horizon. The plane of the observer, marked with dotted lines, passes through the center of the celestial sphere because the Earth's radius is very tiny compared with the size of the celestial sphere. (b) At the equator, the stars move straight up from the horizon. (c) At 45° latitude, the stars follow a path tipped 45° to the horizon. (d) At 45° latitude, the Sun will reach a midday altitude of 45° at the time of an equinox. What will be its altitude at the same time at the equator? At the North Pole? Because stars such as Polaris are so far away, sight lines to them are parallel from all points on Earth.

plane of the equator and perpendicular to the Earth's axis. As a result, all the stars appear to rotate around Polaris as shown in Figure 13a. At the time of the vernal or autumnal equinox, the Sun would move parallel to the horizon. At the summer solstice, the Sun would be visible all day at an altitude of 23.5°; that is, the angle between your line of sight to the Sun and the ground underneath you would be 23.5°. What would happen at the winter solstice?

On the equator, Polaris is on the horizon, and the plane on which you stand is parallel to the Earth's axis. Consequently, the stars move along circular paths whose planes are perpendicular to the Earth's axis and to the plane on which you stand (see Figure 13b). At the time of an equinox, the Sun maps a path from east to west that brings it to the zenith (directly overhead) at midday.

At a latitude of 45°, Polaris is 45° above the northern horizon, and the plane on which you stand is at an angle of 45° to the Earth's axis (see Figure 13c). The stars rise on the eastern horizon and move along arcs that are tilted 45° to the horizon and to the plane on which you stand. At the time of an equinox, the Sun rises due east on the horizon and ascends along an arc that brings it to a midday altitude of 45° (Figure 13d).

Project 11

Describe the path of the Sun across the sky at the time of the summer solstice as seen from (1) the equator; (2) 45° north latitude. Describe the path from the same two positions at the time of the winter solstice.

Project 12

Make a model to show the path of the Sun across the sky as it appears to someone at 45° north latitude at the time of an equinox and at the summer and winter solstices.

Investigation 13: The Motion of the Stars on the Celestial Sphere

As you can see from the photograph on p. 73, the stars near the north celestial pole appear to move along circular paths centered on the pole. Constellations close to the celestial poles are called polar constellations. To viewers at high latitudes, these stars never set. At the North Pole, the visible constellations are polar constellations because they all circle the north celestial pole (see Figure 13a). At the equator, no constellations can be seen all the time (see Figure 13b).

What are the polar constellations where you live? That is, which constellations can you observe circling the North Star? To find out, you need to identify Polaris. It is the last star on the handle of the Little Dipper. To locate it, find the stars of the Big Dipper in the northern sky. They are brighter than Polaris, and the shape of the constellation is very distinct. The best time to locate it is in the evening from January to July. Part of it may be below the horizon in the evening during the autumn and early winter in southern parts of the United States. Figure 14a shows you how to locate Polaris by using the pointer stars, Dubhe and Merak, of the Big Dipper. Figure 14b shows some of the constellations close to Polaris. How can you determine which ones are polar constellations at your latitude?

Watch the polar constellations over a period of a

Monitoring the position of certain constellations in the night sky is one way to keep track of time throughout the year. Stars above the North Pole move in a circular path centered on the North Star, as shown in this long-exposure photograph.

year. Do they appear to rotate clockwise or counter-clockwise around Polaris? Can you explain why?

As you saw in Figure 13d, Polaris appears at the same altitude as the latitude from which it is viewed. To see if this holds true for the latitude where you live, build an astrolabe, as shown in Figure 15, and measure

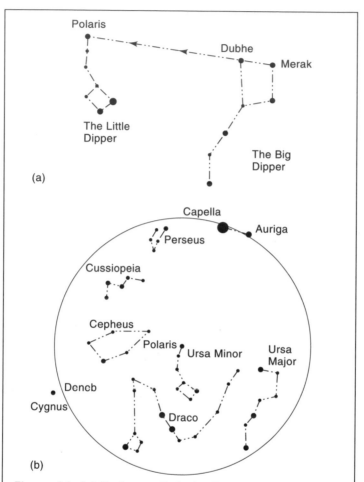

Figure 14. (a) To locate Polaris, find the Big Dipper. The pointer stars Dubhe and Merak form a line that points close to Polaris, at the tip of the Little Dipper. The distance from Dubhe to Polaris is about five times the distance from Merak to Dubhe. Place your thumb and index finger next to the pointer stars to gauge their distance, and then mark off five of those measurements to Polaris. (b) This is a view from the North Pole of some of the constellations near Polaris. Which ones are polar constellations at your latitude?

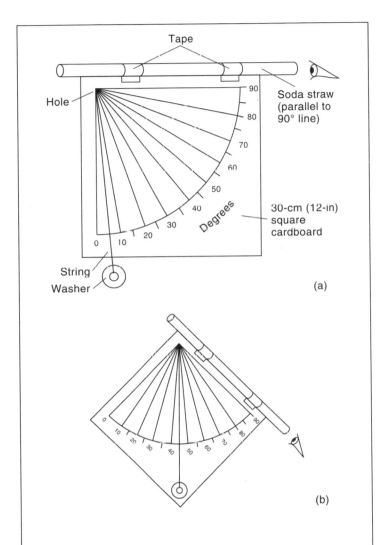

Figure 15. (a) To measure the altitude of a star or the moon, make an astrolabe as shown. Use a protractor to draw the angle markings. Thread the end of the string through the hole and tape it to the back of the cardboard. (b) To use the astrolabe, point the straw toward a star or the moon. *Do not use it to look at the Sun.* The position of the string will mark the altitude in degrees.

the angle of Polaris with respect to the ground. What do you find its altitude to be? How does this compare with your latitude?

Other constellations such as Orion, Canis Major, and Sagittarius are too far from Polaris to be polar constellations. Describe the path of these constellations across the celestial hemisphere.

Watch a single nonpolar constellation for several months. Does its rising time become earlier or later over the course of weeks and months? Does it move eastward or westward with time? Can you explain why?

Like the paths of the Sun and planets, the moon's path lies along the ecliptic. But the moon makes one revolution every month. At full moon, why must the moon and the Sun be on opposite sides of the ecliptic? Keeping these positions in mind, at what point along the horizon would you expect a full moon to rise at a time close to an equinox? At a time close to the summer solstice? At a time close to the winter solstice? Test your predictions by watching the position of the full moon as it rises at these times of the year. Were your predictions correct?

Project 13

Develop a geometric proof to show that the altitude of Polaris is equal to the latitude where it is observed for any latitude in the Northern Hemisphere.

WHAT IS A DAY?

You may be surprised to learn that your day is not the same as an astronomer's day. One complete rotation of the Earth, as you can see from Figure 16, brings a point on the Earth back to the same celestial meridian. That means a star that was on a meridian at noon yesterday will be there again after exactly one rotation. However, if the Sun were on that same meridian yesterday, it will not be there one rotation later. As the Earth rotates, it also moves along its orbit. In 1 day, it travels almost 1 degree (actually $360°/365.25$ days) along this path. Consequently, the Earth must make slightly more than one rotation before the Sun is again overhead. This extra degree or so of rotation takes about 4 minutes, making the Sun appear to move eastward by about 1 degree each day.

Project 14
Show that 1 degree of rotation by the Earth takes 4 minutes.

Astronomers are generally more interested in the time for the Earth to make one rotation: that is, the time between successive passages of the same star over a fixed meridian. As you've seen, this period, which is known as the *sidereal day*, is approximately 4 minutes less than the solar day—the time it takes the Sun to return to a fixed meridian.

The problem with solar days is they are not exactly the same from one part of the year to the next. There are two reasons for this. First, the Earth's orbit is not a perfect circle; it is slightly elliptical. Although the elliptical shape is exaggerated in Figure 17a, the drawing shows that the Earth travels fastest when it is closest to the Sun (in January) and slowest when it is farthest from the Sun (in July). As a result, the Earth must turn

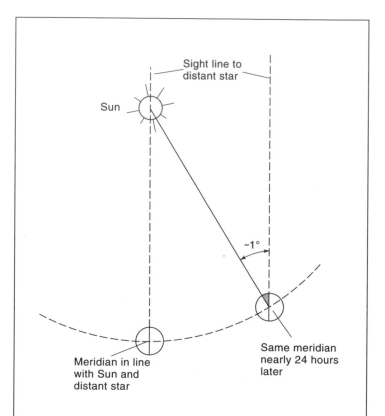

Figure 16. After one rotation of the Earth, the Sun does not appear in exactly the same spot in the sky as it did before. This diagram, which is not to scale, shows why. A meridian initially in line with both the Sun and a star will still be in line with the star after one rotation, but not with the Sun. The shift is caused by the Earth's movement around the Sun. As a result of the movment, the Sun reaches the same meridian, or the same spot in the sky, about 4 minutes later each day. Therefore, one rotation of the Earth actually takes 4 minutes less than 24 hours.

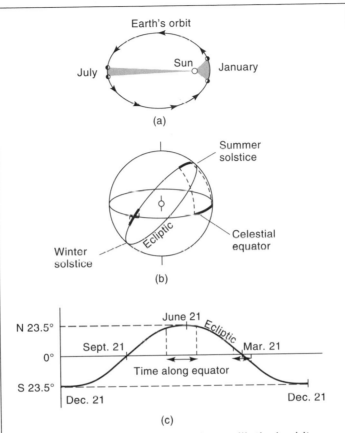

Figure 17. (a) The Earth moves in an elliptical orbit. (b) At the solstices, the movement of the Sun along the ecliptic is nearly parallel to the celestial equator, as can be seen by looking at the pair of highlighted segments to the right in the celestial sphere. The pair of segments to the left show that during times close to the equinoxes, a considerable part of the Sun's motion is northward or southward rather than eastward along the equator. (c) Another way of showing this effect is to graph the Sun's latitude on the celestial sphere as a function of time as the Sun moves along the ecliptic.

slightly more than average (slightly more than 1 revolution + 360/365.25 degree) for the Sun to make successive passages across a fixed meridian in January and slightly less than average in July.

The second reason for unequal solar days has to do with the Sun's apparent movement along the ecliptic. Near the summer and winter solstices, the Sun's motion on the ecliptic is nearly parallel to the celestial equator as you can see in Figure 17b, but at the time of the equinoxes, a significant part of the Sun's motion is north or south rather than parallel to the equator. As a result, the amount the Earth must rotate before the Sun returns to a fixed meridian varies from day to day.

To allow humans to enjoy uniform time, not having to reset their clocks and watches each day, astronomers invented an imaginary Sun—the *mean sun*. The mean sun moves along the celestial equator at a uniform rate equivalent to the average speed of the Sun along its path. Sometimes the mean sun is slightly ahead of the real Sun; sometimes it is slightly behind.

The mean solar day, which is tracked by our clocks, is exactly 24 hours long. Noon during the mean solar day may differ from the time when the Sun reaches its peak altitude by as much as 16 minutes. The period from one peak altitude of the Sun to the next is called the apparent solar day. For a modern society more geared to the clock than to the Sun, the mean solar day is much more convenient than the apparent solar day, which is forever changing.

Investigation 14: Making an Analemma

You can see how the mean solar day differs from the apparent solar day by mapping the Sun's position at exactly the same clock time every day. To do this, cover the lower pane of a south-facing window with a sheet of cardboard. Tape a sheet of paper to a table or counter near the bottom of the cardboard. Remove the cardboard and with a nail, make a hole through it about 10 cm (4 in) above where the paper will be when you return the cardboard to the window.

Sunlight coming through the hole will make a bright spot on the paper. At exactly noon, mark the center of the bright spot on the paper with a pen or pencil. Do this at noon on every sunny day. It doesn't matter if you miss a few days. In fact, as long as you mark the Sun at exactly noon by your clock at least once a week, you will be able to see a pattern develop over the course of a few months. If you carry on the experiment for a year, you will obtain a figure-eight pattern that resembles the analemma found on many globes and sundials.

Why does the spot move farther from the window during the winter and closer during the summer? As you can see, the spots do not lie along a straight north-south line even though they were marked at exactly the same time each day. What does this tell you about the Sun's position in the sky? During which weeks of the year does the Sun move ahead of the clock, or mean solar time? During which weeks of the year is Sun time behind clock time? How does your pattern of spots compare with the analemma seen on the globe in the photograph on p. 82?

TIME ZONES

Until the late nineteenth century, residents in each United States community set their clocks or watches by

The analemma, shaped like a figure eight, marks the latitude of the Sun's position above the Earth for each day of the year. It also indicates how many minutes a clock runs ahead of or behind the Sun at midday for that day.

the Sun. Noon was the time when the Sun reached its peak altitude for the day. They knew the Sun had peaked when it lay in the direction of due south. There was really no need for greater accuracy.

But the arrival of train travel changed all that. By the last quarter of that century, railroad companies had more than a thousand trains moving along more than

100,000 miles of track. Trying to prepare or follow a train schedule was nearly impossible because each station had a different time. When clocks in Albany, New York, read 12 o'clock noon, the hands of clocks in Buffalo, New York, indicated approximately 11:40, and clocks in Syracuse, New York, read 11:50. In addition, as you have found, noon according to apparent solar time varies from day to day so clocks had to be reset every few days.

On October 11, 1883, in an effort to reduce the confusion associated with time differences between stations, American railroad companies agreed to divide the United States into four time zones. The zones were similar, though not identical, to our present time zones,

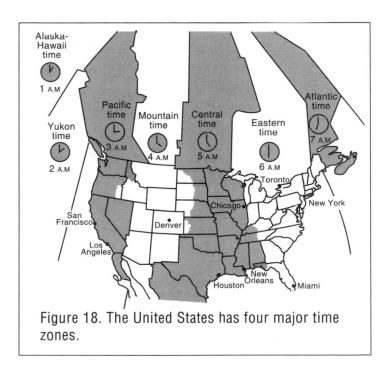

Figure 18. The United States has four major time zones.

shown in Figure 18. As you can see, the boundaries of time zones do not exactly parallel the lines of longitude. As a matter of convenience, the lines sometimes follow state boundaries or rivers. At noon on November 8, 1883, all railroad clocks were reset to the noon reading for clocks at the middle of the time zone. To coordinate the setting of clocks, a telegraph signal was sent to different stations across the country.

Although time zones are a great convenience for business, transportation, and communication, it was not until March 19, 1918, that Congress passed the Standard Time Act making time within the four time zones the official time for the entire nation. The same act started Daylight Saving Time (DST) on March 30, 1918. Its purpose was to provide an additional hour of light at the end of the day in summer to reduce energy use.

DST was not popular with American farmers, who preferred the hour of light in the early morning when much of their work was done. It was discontinued after World War I. However, it was reinstated in World War II and has remained in effect in many states. Generally, in those states where DST is mandated, clocks are advanced 1 hour on the last Sunday in April. These same states return to standard time on the last Sunday in October.

You know from experience that the Sun appears to move from east to west, which is equivalent to the Earth's rotating from west to east. With that in mind use Figure 18 to determine what time it is in Houston when it's 10 A.M. in New York City. At the same moment, what time is it in Denver? In San Francisco? In Miami?

Figure 19 shows the time zones around the entire Northern Hemisphere. You can see that time zone

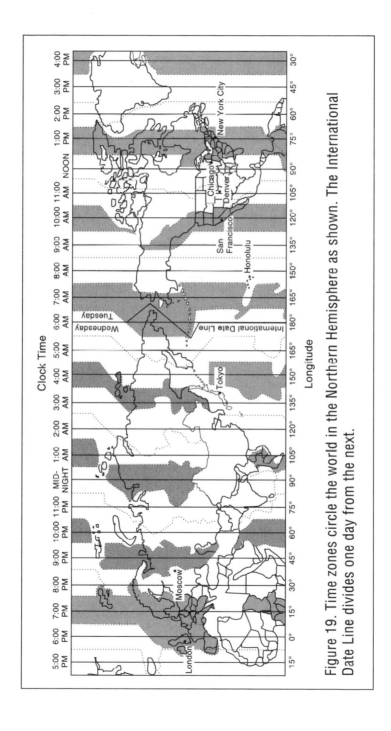

Figure 19. Time zones circle the world in the Northern Hemisphere as shown. The International Date Line divides one day from the next.

boundaries in other countries are not always parallel to longitudinal lines either. Notice, too, the International Date Line that runs in a north-south direction across the Pacific Ocean. When you cross that line going from east to west, you add a day to the calendar. If it's 6:00 A.M. on Tuesday, July 10, east of the International Date Line, it's 6:00 A.M. on Wednesday, July 11, west of the line. What happens when you travel from west to east across the same line?

To convince yourself that the International Date Line makes sense, start at New York City at 1:00 P.M. on Tuesday (see Figure 19) and move west on a quick "map trip" through the time zones. Don't forget to add a day when you cross the International Date Line, and remember, a new day begins at midnight. What day and time is it when you get back to New York?

Project 15

Suppose you live in Denver, Colorado, and you have friends in New York, Chicago, San Francisco, Honolulu, Tokyo, Moscow, and London. You decide to call each friend on January 1 at 12:01 their time to wish them a Happy New Year. At what time and on what day (your time) would you place each call?

Investigation 15: A Shadow Clock

The first clock hand was probably the shadow of a stick on the ground. To build a simple shadow clock, cover a 50-cm (20-in) square board with paper. Use a small lump of clay to hold a pencil or stick, about 10 cm (4 in) in length, in a vertical position near the midpoint of the south side of the board (see Figure 20). The stick is often referred to as a *gnomon*. Place the board in a level, sunny area early in the morning.

Mark the tip of the gnomon's shadow on the paper every hour or so as the Sun moves across the sky. Note the clock time in your notebook whenever you make a mark. Later, you can draw lines connecting the marks to the base of the stick. Continue to mark the end of the gnomon's shadow periodically until sunset.

As you know, the time of midday—the time when the Sun reaches its maximum altitude—depends on where you live in your time zone. Noon on a clock, or 1:00 P.M. DST, is not necessarily midday according to the Sun. To pinpoint midday, drive a stick about 40 cm (16 in) long into the ground at the north side of the

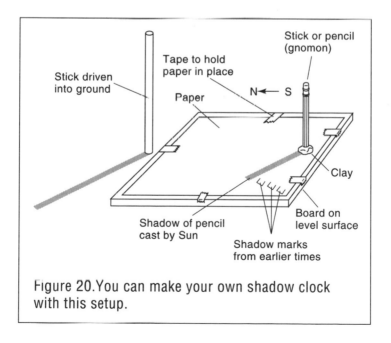

Figure 20. You can make your own shadow clock with this setup.

board as shown in Figure 20. You might do this soon after you begin marking the tips of the gnomon's shadow. Use a carpenter's level to make sure the stick is vertical.

About an hour before midday, use a string and a small stick to scratch a semicircle as shown in Figure 21 around the stick you drove into the ground. Let the radius of the semicircle be the length of the stick's shadow. Mark the spot where the shadow touches the circle. Why will the shadow continue to grow shorter as midday approaches?

When the Sun moves close to its maximum altitude, mark the end of the shadow frequently. As the shadow lengthens after midday, continue to watch it

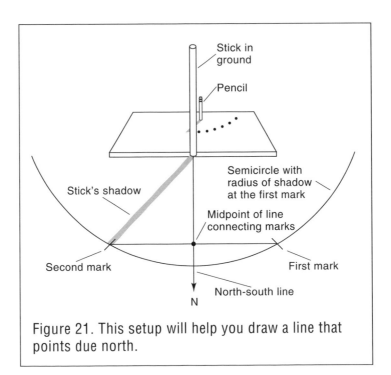

Figure 21. This setup will help you draw a line that points due north.

until it again touches the semicircle you scratched on the ground. Mark the point where the shadow touches the circle and draw a straight line between the two marks on the circle. Make a third mark at the center of the line you drew. Where is this midpoint in relation to the position of the stick's shortest shadow? In what geographical direction was the Sun when the stick cast the shortest shadow? What is the direction of a line drawn from the stick to the center of the straight line you drew across the semicircle? Save this line and the stick. You will need them for Investigations 16 and 17.

This shadow clock was used by Egyptians in about 1000 B.C.

By the end of the day, you will have a line that points due north and a series of lines marking shadows that fell on the paper throughout the day. How could you use the shadow lines to make a clock that could measure time? Remember, shadow clocks were invented long before mechanical clocks. In what part of the world would you guess shadow clocks were first used?

Mark the lines with the actual clock time when the gnomon's shadow fell on them. Or, to make sure the readings are correct, calibrate the lines with a clock or watch the next day. Test your shadow clock at various times throughout the year. Are the time lines you calibrated earlier valid at other times of the year?

Investigation 16: A Sundial

At some point in history, it was discovered that the direction of a shadow cast by a gnomon slanting at an angle parallel to the Earth's axis was the same at any given hour of the day regardless of the season. This discovery led to sundials, which are much more accurate timekeepers than shadow clocks. (Project 16 will help you to see that the shadows are cast at the same angle in every season.)

You can make a sundial so that you can see this for yourself. To obtain the widest time range, the sundial should be built in the summer when the Sun is in the sky the longest. First, you must find the latitude of your home. You can make a reasonable estimate from a map or globe. As you can see if you look back at Figure 13, the latitude is equivalent to the angle the Earth's axis makes with the ground's surface at that latitude. Therefore, the dial's gnomon should slant at an angle equal to the latitude.

A thick board about 30 cm (12 in) on a side can serve as the base of your sundial. Instead of a stick, the gnomon will be a flat board slanted at the appropriate angle as shown in Figure 22. Ask an adult to help you cut the gnomon from a board that is about 2 cm (3/4 in) thick. Glue the gnomon to the base, supporting the gnomon vertically with blocks or clamps until the glue dries. You may want to paint the base white to increase the visibility of the lines you will draw on it later.

On a sunny day at a few minutes before midday, place the sundial near the north-south line you estab-

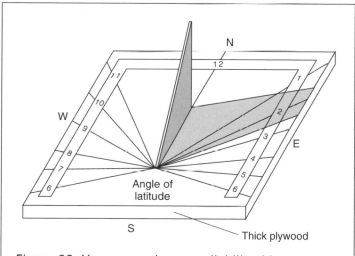

Figure 22. You can make a sundial like this one from wood. Be sure the angle of the gnomon equals your latitude. What time is it, according to this sundial?

lished during Investigation 15. At precisely midday, when the stick's shadow lies on the north-south line, place the dial so that the gnomon's shadow points due north. In this position, there should be no shadow on either side of the gnomon because the shadow falls behind and in line with the gnomon. A line through the center of the shadow on the dial can be marked "12." By how many minutes does local solar noon (midday) differ from noon on your watch or clock?

Exactly 1 hour later, draw a line along the shadow cast by the sloping edge of the gnomon. Label this line with a "1." Continue to mark lines in this way at 1-hour intervals until sunset. You now have all the lines you need to calibrate a sundial that will measure *sun time*. Why may the lines on your sundial not agree with clock time? How could you make clock and dial times agree?

To draw the lines for the morning hours, you may simply draw a mirror image of the afternoon lines on the other side of the gnomon. For example, measure the angle between the gnomon and the 1:00 P.M. line and mark off the same angle between the gnomon and the 11:00 A.M. line on the other side. The 10:00 A.M. line will make the same angle as the 2:00 P.M. line and so on.

Just before midday the next day, place your sundial on level ground and at midday, adjust it as before so that the gnomon points north. You might want to mount it permanently to a post, wall, or patio.

Check your sundial periodically throughout the year. Why do the times not always agree perfectly with the first Sun-time lines you drew?

The first sundial builders had no clocks to deter-

Portable sundials that incorporated compasses were used for timekeeping as late as the eighteenth century.

mine their hour lines. How do you think they calibrated their dials? Doing Project 16 may help you understand how the first dials were calibrated, but the process is very time-consuming. That is why you were asked to use a clock in this investigation.

Project 16
Use the information in Table 3 to show that the shadow cast by a sundial will lie along the same

TABLE 3: The Sun's Altitude and Azimuth at 40° Latitude

Date	Solar Time	Altitude (°)	Azimuth (°)
March 21	10 a.m.	41.6	41.9
June 21	10 a.m.	59.8	65.8
October 21	10 a.m.	32.4	35.6
December 21	10 a.m.	20.7	29.4

line at the same time of day regardless of the season. The table gives the Sun's position for latitude 40° at 10 A.M. on the four dates that start a new season. The altitude is the angle of the Sun above the horizon; the azimuth is the angle of the Sun east of a line that points due south.

Investigation 17: A Global View of Our Globe

To obtain a more global perspective of the Earth as seen from a spaceship, place a globe outside in a spot where the Sun will shine on it all day. A point near the north-south line you drew in Investigation 15 might be a good choice.

Remove the globe from its usual support and place it on a large empty can as shown in the photograph. Turn the globe so that your location is uppermost. Mark the location with a pin, inserting it into a small piece of clay attached to the globe. Keeping your town at the top, turn the globe so that its axis lies along a north-south line. Why will the globe's north pole now point toward Polaris? (Refer again to Figure 13d)

Study the globe carefully. Where is the Sun rising

If the white-tipped pin on top of this globe represents
your location on the Earth, and the globe's axis is
aligned from north to south along the Earth, then the
North Pole of the globe will point toward the North Star.

at this moment? Where is it setting? Which continents and cities are in darkness? Are there places near either pole where the Sun will not set today? Are there places near a pole that will be in darkness all day? What time is it at this moment in Chicago? New York? San Francisco? Honolulu? Tokyo? New Delhi? Berlin? London?

You can locate the place on Earth where the Sun is directly overhead at this moment. To do so, cut off a short piece of a soda straw and stick a pin through it. Recall that a vertical stick will not cast a shadow when the Sun is directly above it. Keeping the straw perpendicular to the globe's surface, move the straw along the globe until you find a place where the Sun shines straight down the straw and casts no shadow. Where is the Sun directly overhead at this moment?

Note the latitude and longitude of this place and try to predict where the Sun will be directly overhead 1 hour from now. Two hours from now.

Return to the globe at those times and test your predictions. Were you correct?

How can you add a moon to your model? Where would the moon be at this moment in your model if it were to rise tonight as a full moon? As a new crescent moon? If it is visible in the sky right now?

Repeat your observations using this model at different times of the year. What changes occur as the seasons change?

TIME
AND
CLOCKS

Clocks and watches are so common today that we tend to think they were strapped to the wrists of the first primates who walked erect. But, in fact, clocks as we know them have existed for only about 600 years. Mechanical clocks were preceded by a number of other timekeeping devices such as water clocks, hourglasses, and burning timers such as candles and oil lamps.

As you've seen, ancient Egyptians could measure the passage of time during the day with a shadow clock. It was a simple matter for them to divide the day into hours based on the movement of a stick's shadow through equal angles. The hours would not all have been of equal time, but precisely equal intervals were not essential to Egyptian culture. To divide the night into time intervals, they used water clocks, also known as *clepsydras*.

A water clock appears to be a very simple timekeeping device. Water flows or drips from a hole at the bottom of one vessel into another. The volume of water

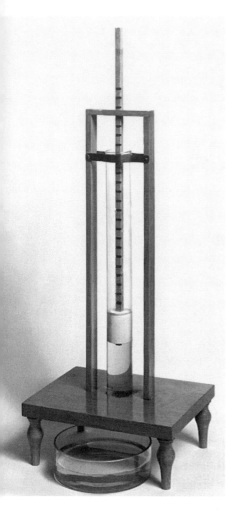

Before the invention of mechanical clocks, Arabians used this water clock to measure time. Water runs out through a hole in the bottom of the cylinder into the dish below. As the graduated stick drops, the marks move by the bar, indicating the passage of a specific amount of time.

that collects in the second container is a measure of time. Alternatively, water may flow into a floating air-filled vessel with a small hole on top. As air is replaced by water, the vessel sinks. Time is measured by the distance the vessel has sunk according to marks along the side of the vessel.

Still another approach was to measure the rise of a float in a vessel into which water flowed at a uniform rate. Some designers of clepsydras connected the floats to gears that rotated a clock hand to indicate the hour. This was the forerunner of the clock face.

Investigation 18: Water Clocks

Although the principle of the water clock is quite simple, building a good one is difficult, as you will see. Make a hole in the bottom of a polystyrene plastic (Styrofoam) coffee cup by pushing a small nail through from the inside to the outside. If you do not have a 100-ml graduated cylinder, make one by attaching a piece of masking tape to the side of a clear cylindrical jar. With a marking pen, make lines on the tape at 1-cm or smaller intervals starting from the bottom of the cylinder. Why does the space between the lines on the cylindrical jar correspond to equal volumes?

To support the coffee cup, put two small sticks or toothpicks across the mouth of your graduated cylinder as shown in Figure 23a. Get a partner with a clock or a watch that can measure time in seconds. Then place your finger over the hole on the bottom of the cup as you fill it with water. Have your partner begin timing

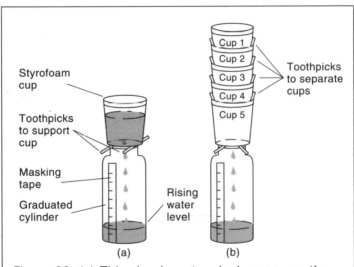

Figure 23. (a) This simple water clock measures the time it takes water to drip into a graduated cylinder or jar. (b) A more sophisticated water clock equalizes the time it takes each unit of water to fall.

when you place the cup on the graduated cylinder. Record the time it takes the water level in the cylinder to reach the first line, the second line, the third line, and so on.

What happens to the time required for equal volumes of water to flow as the water level in the coffee cup falls? What is wrong with this simple water clock? Can you explain why?

To see how the time for water to empty from a container is related to the height, or head, of the water in the vessel, ask an adult to help you make a hole in the bottom of a coffee can with a small nail. Pliers can be used to push the nail through the can from the inside to the outside. Wear gloves to prevent scratches. Put your finger over the hole in the can and fill it nearly full with water over a sink. Have your partner measure the height of the water in the can with a ruler. Then remove your finger while your partner measures the time it takes for all the water to flow from the can. Record the water height and the emptying time.

Refill the can to lesser heights and repeat the experiment several times. Be sure to record the initial height of the water and the emptying time for each trial.

To see the relationship between the two quantities, plot a graph of emptying time versus the initial height of the water. What does the graph tell you? Is the emptying time proportional to the height of the water in the can?

Try plotting emptying time versus the *square root* of the initial height of the water. What does this graph tell you? How does it help explain the problem with the simple water clock you constructed?

A small-scale version of one ancient solution to the problem of building a water clock is shown in Figure 23b. The bottom of each cup has a small hole through it. The small sticks or toothpicks in between the cups hold them apart to prevent an air lock. Build and test this water clock. Does it measure equal time intervals? Can you build a better water clock? What could you do to maintain a constant head of water?

THE SANDS OF TIME

The hourglass or sandglass might be thought of as a solid-state water clock; instead of water, solid particles mark the time. The sandglass was used in ancient Greece as it is today to measure relatively short time intervals such as the time to boil an egg. Larger sandglasses for timing classes in schools and sermons in church appeared during the Middle Ages. Because they measured approximately 1/24 of a day, these sandclocks may be correctly called hourglasses.

The particles flowing in an hourglass may be marble dust or powdered egg shells as well as fine sand. Before it is placed in the hourglass, the material is passed through a series of fine sieves to be certain the particles are all very nearly the same size. The hole through which the particles fall is usually about ten times the diameter of the particles.

Investigation 19: How Precise and Accurate Is a Sandclock?

Find a sandglass to experiment with. There may be one in your kitchen to measure the time to boil an egg.

These sandglasses from the eighteenth century measure 15 minutes, one-half hour, 45 minutes, and an hour.

Many games that set a time limit, such as Pictionary®, contain sandglasses. Use a stopwatch or a clock with a second hand to find out how long it takes the sand to flow through the narrow opening connecting the upper half of the "hourglass" with the lower half. Do this several times and record the actual time the sand flows for each trial. Then determine the average time from all your trials.

Usually, sandglasses found in games or in the kitchen are designed to measure a period of 1, 2, or 3 minutes. The game's directions or the instructions on the cooking timer should indicate the interval it measures.

How accurate is the sandglass? That is, how closely does the average time for the sand to flow from upper to lower level compare with the time it is supposed to measure? For example, if it takes 54 seconds for the sand to flow through a 1-minute timer, then the timer's accuracy is within 10 percent of what it claims to measure. What is the accuracy of the sandglass you're using?

To find the precision of the instrument, you must know the range of the times you measured. For example, if your measurements in seconds were 53, 54, 55, 53, and 55, then the sandglass measures time to 54 ± 1 seconds. It covers a range of 2 seconds, which means it has a precision of 2 percent. Thus, the sandglass is quite precise, even though it's not very accurate. What is the precision of your sandglass?

Investigation 20: Building a Sandglass

To make a sandglass, you'll need two identical glass jars, such as baby food jars and some fine, dry sand or table salt. The jars and the sand or salt must be very dry. If they are not, put them in a warm oven for about an hour. Then pour the sand or salt into one of the jars until it is almost full.

With scissors, cut a circular piece of heavy paper or light cardboard to fit the mouth of the jar. Make a hole with a paper punch in the center of the paper and place it on the mouth of the jar. Invert the empty jar and set it on top of the paper. Then tape the mouths of the jars firmly together.

Turn the jars over and watch the solid fall into the lower jar. What interval of time does your sandglass measure? How precise is your timer? How can you adjust it to measure a particular length of time? How accurate is it? How would you go about building an hourglass timer (one that measures a period of 1 hour)?

ONE CANDLE PAST MIDNIGHT

Oil lamps and candles have also been used as time-keepers. The passage of time was marked in a burning oil lamp by the falling level of oil in its reservoir. The reservoir was made of transparent glass so that the oil could be seen, and it was calibrated with marks to indicate time according to oil level. The rate that an oil lamp burns depends on the height of the wick exposed to the air; consequently, the wick had to be adjusted carefully before the lamp was lit.

A candle will burn quite uniformly in a room where there are no drafts. The height of a candle has been used in the past as a measure of time. At English auctions, for example, a pin was often stuck in the side of a lighted candle. When the pin fell, the person holding the bid at that moment was considered the buyer.

This candle clock from the beginning of the nineteenth century marks the passage of 1 hour as it burns from one round node to the next.

Project 17

Under adult supervision, design and build a "candle clock." How accurate is your clock? How precise is it?

MECHANICAL CLOCKS

The origin of the mechanical clock is unknown, but by the fourteenth century several clocks driven by falling weights existed in Europe. The weights turned a horizontal shaft as shown in Figure 24. A toothed wheel attached to the shaft turned with it, but only one tooth at a time, thanks to a regulating device known as an *escapement*. This device is characteristic of all mechanical clocks.

The escapement consisted of a vertical shaft called a *verge* with two stops that alternately engaged the teeth at the top and bottom of the wheel. As the teeth pushed against a stop, the verge rotated with the wheel until the stop "escaped" the wheel. Then the other stop engaged

A wall clock from the fourteenth century is regulated
by a verge and foliot escapement mechanism. The
verge is the thin vertical rod and the foliot is the
horizontal bar with weights near the top of the verge.

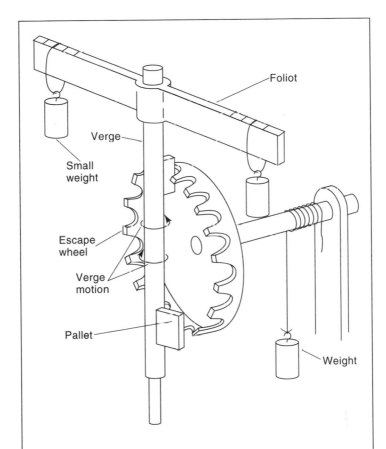

Foliot

Verge

Small
weight

Escape
wheel

Verge
motion

Pallet

Weight

Figure 24. In early mechanical clocks, a weight was
used to turn the escape wheel. To keep the wheel
turning very slowly, the two pallets on the verge inter-
rupt the wheel's motion by alternately engaging with
teeth on its rim. The pallets, or stops, intermittently
"escape" the wheel, letting it turn a notch before it
hits the other pallet. As a result, the verge rotates
back and forth. The rate of its motion is controlled by
the size of the falling weight and by the foliot, which
pivots on top of the verge. The size of the small
weights on either end of the foliot and their distance
from the pivot point affect the speed of the verge.

and the wheel briefly stopped turning. Thus, the wheel, moving very slowly and evenly, could track time.

The rate of back-and-forth motion of the verge was controlled by a bar called a *foliot* that pivoted on top of the verge. Small weights on either end of the foliot could be moved along the bar to change the speed of the clock. Early clocks often had a means of striking a hammer against a loud bell so that inhabitants of a town could mark the passage of hours. Many did not have dials, but those that did usually had only one hand, the hour hand, to indicate time.

When such clocks stopped, they were reset according to a sundial because at that time it was a more accurate timekeeper than the clock. In fact, mechanical clocks were initially so inaccurate that they were accompanied by sundials for setting the clocks. The direction the hands of modern clocks turn—the direction we call clockwise—is believed to originate from the direction a sundial's shadow moves in the Northern Hemisphere.

Mechanical clocks improved with the replacement of the foliot by a swinging pendulum to control the escapement, as shown in Figure 25. Although Leonardo da Vinci's notes from around 1500 contain an idea for a pendulum clock, Galileo Galilei, who lived about a century later, is generally credited with making the first one. A number of other people modified and improved Galileo's invention.

Investigation 21: Time and the Pendulum

One of Galileo's earliest discoveries took place in a church. Unable to concentrate on the sermon, he watched a chandelier, driven by air currents, swing

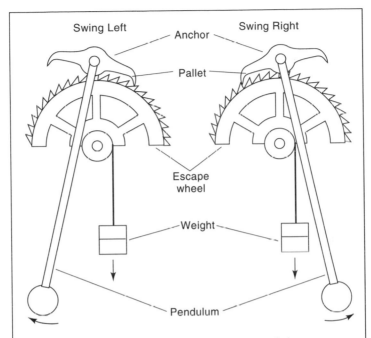

Figure 25. A pendulum clock uses a pendulum instead of a verge and foliot to control the rotation of an escape wheel. The swinging pendulum rocks an anchor back and forth as shown so that the pallets at each end of the anchor alternately engage the teeth on the escape wheel. With each swing, the escape wheel and the pallets disengage for a short period and the wheel, driven by the weight, moves by one tooth. The force of the teeth on the pallets keeps the pendulum swinging.

through arcs of different lengths. Using his pulse as a timer, he found that the time it took the chandelier to swing back and forth appeared to be independent of the arc length.

When the service was over, he began a more careful investigation of the pendulum using a water clock.

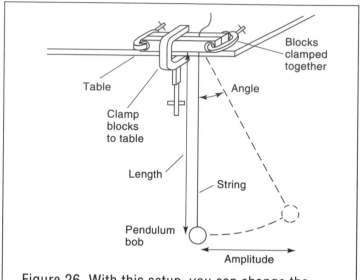

Table

Clamp
blocks
to table

Length

Pendulum
bob

Blocks
clamped
together

Angle

String

Amplitude

Figure 26. With this setup, you can change the amplitude and length of a pendulum, as well as the weight of its bob.

For your investigation, you may prefer to use a stop-watch or a clock with a second hand. Galileo didn't have that option. There were no mechanical devices in the sixteenth century to measure short time intervals.

Use a long string to make a pendulum that has a bob on its lower end as shown in Figure 26. The bob can be a weight with a hook on it or a heavy washer. The upper end of the string can be held firmly in place by clamping two small blocks of wood together, one on either side of the string. Clamp these blocks to a table, the top of a door frame, or some other place where the pendulum can swing freely. To test this, pull the bob a short distance to one side and release it.

The length of the pendulum can be changed by

pulling the string between the wood blocks when the clamps are loosened slightly. A less sturdy pendulum can be made by taping the string to a door frame or ceiling joist. To begin, make a pendulum that is about a meter (3.3 ft.) long.

The amplitude of the pendulum is half the distance the bob moves, or the distance from one end of its swing to the middle. The pendulum's period is the time it takes the bob to make one complete swing over and back. You can check Galileo's idea that the period is independent of the amplitude by measuring the period of your pendulum.

Why will it be more accurate to measure the time it takes to make 50 or 100 complete swings, rather than just one? How long does it take the pendulum to make 50 complete swings? To make 100 complete swings? Is the period of a pendulum constant? What can you do to find out if Galileo was right about the period being independent of the amplitude?

Does the weight of the bob affect the period of the pendulum? To find out, vary the weight of the bob and measure the period. You can use two washers instead of one, or use a 200-gram (7-ounce) weight instead of a 100-gram (3.5-ounce) weight. To be sure that the length of the pendulum does not change, always measure the length of the pendulum from the point of support (where the string is clamped) to the *center* of the weight. Does the weight of the bob affect the period of the pendulum?

Does a pendulum's length affect its period? Does the period double when the length doubles? To find out how the period is related to length, measure the period when the pendulum's length, in meters, is 0.25 m, 0.50

m, 0.75 m, 1.00 m, 1.50 m, and, if possible, 2.00 m (or 10 in, 20 in, 30 in, 40 in, 60 in, and 80 in).

Galileo found that the square of a pendulum's period is proportional to its length; that is,

$$T^2 = kL,$$

where T is the period, L is the length, and k is a proportionality constant.

To find out if your results agree with Galileo's, plot a graph of the pendulum's period squared (T^2) as a function of its length (L); that is, plot T^2 on the vertical axis and L on the horizontal axis. Do the points of your graph lie very close to a straight line? If so, what do you conclude?

What is the slope (rise/run) of your graph? What is the significance of the slope? How can you use the slope to determine k, the proportionality constant?

Use what you have learned to predict the length of a pendulum that has a period of one second. Then build the pendulum and test your prediction. Were you right? Can you figure out a way to make a pendulum that has a period of $1/2$ second? Of $1/4$ second?

How did clock makers use Galileo's discovery? What additional factors did they have to consider to make a practical clock?

BETTER CLOCKS

From the late seventeenth century onward, there were dramatic improvements in clock making. Metal-cutting machines could make very accurate escape wheels with

**The steady swing of a pendulum
regulates the timing of this clock.**

many identical teeth. Better anchors and escapement mechanisms were devised. And methods were introduced to prevent the expansion and contraction of metal pendulums caused by temperature changes. As the nineteenth century drew to a close, the French physicist

Charles-Edouard Guillaume discovered that an alloy of iron and nickel changed very little in length over a wide range of temperatures. Guillaume named the alloy *invar*, for "invariable," because of its virtually constant size.

SPRINGS AND TIME

Clocks driven by coiled springs appeared late in the fifteenth century. Such clocks could be made much smaller than weight-driven timepieces. In fact, clocks small enough to be carried in pockets—watches—were in evidence a century later. The first wristwatch arrived in 1790 as an adornment of a woman's bracelet. Then, in 1880, the German navy developed a small watch that

When springs replaced weights for driving timepieces, pocket watches became possible. The coil spring and gears of this pocket watch fit compactly behind the watch face.

officers could strap to their wrists. The value and convenience of wristwatches were firmly established by soldiers who wore them in World War I. They became quite popular among both men and women during the 1920s.

In a spring-driven timepiece, a spring rather than a falling weight drives the gears that turn the minute and hour hands. As shown in Figure 27, a balance wheel and hairspring control the speed of the mechanism, just as a pendulum did in older clocks. The hairspring drives the balance wheel so that it oscillates like a pendulum, causing the lever to pivot back and forth. Pallets at the end of the lever release the escape wheel one tooth at a time. The hairspring is repeatedly rewound by the force of the escape wheel teeth pushing back on the lever.

Project 18
Examine a digital watch or clock. Notice the seven segments that light up in different combinations to form each digit. How do they indicate any time from 1:00 to 12:59?

Investigation 22: A Spring Pendulum
The period of a pendulum, as you found in the previous investigation, is not affected by the mass of its bob. Rather, it is proportional to the square root of its length. You've also read about the hairspring that controls the escapement of a spring-driven clock. You can see the oscillating nature of a spring on a larger scale by examining a spring from a screen door or a window shade.

Hang one end of the spring from a hook or a nail, and attach a mass to the lower end of the spring. Lift the

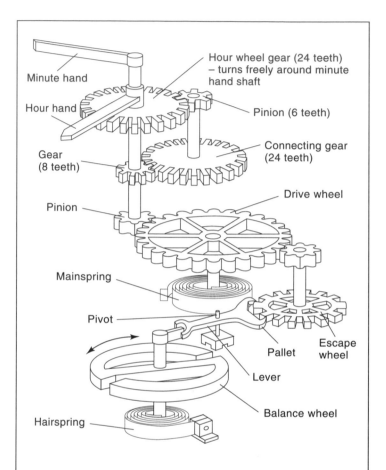

Minute hand

Hour wheel gear (24 teeth)
– turns freely around minute
hand shaft

Hour hand

Pinion (6 teeth)

Gear
(8 teeth)

Connecting gear
(24 teeth)

Pinion

Drive wheel

Mainspring

Pivot

Escape
wheel

Pallet

Lever

Balance wheel

Hairspring

Figure 27. In a spring-type clock or watch, a main spring, which must be wound periodically, turns the drive wheel. The train of gears to the right of the drive wheel controls its rate of rotation through an escapement mechanism. As a result, the drive wheel turns the pinion gear to the left once per hour. The pinion's shaft is connected directly to the minute hand. Another gear on this shaft drives another shaft and the hour wheel gear. The hour hand turns 1/12 as fast as the minute hand shaft. Try to figure out what makes it turn at this rate. How could a second hand be added to this clock?

mass a short distance above its rest position and release it. You'll see that the mass bounces up and down in rhythmic fashion. Is the period of the bouncing mass constant?

Is the period of the oscillating spring, like the period of a pendulum, independent of the mass? If not, how is the period related to the mass? Do different springs have the same period if they support the same mass?

CLOCKS AND LONGITUDE

Early navigators on ships at sea could determine their latitude by measuring the altitude of Polaris or the Sun. But determining longitude was a far more difficult task without good clocks. Clocks allowed navigators to keep track of the time at the ship's port of origin. Then to find the longitude, they only had to compare port time to the time at the ship. Ship time came from the east-west altitude of the Sun or a star.

Without clocks, navigators did the best they could to calculate longitude on the basis of the distance the ship had traveled east or west from their port. They kept track of direction by using a compass and the stars. Near the port's shore, a sailor would drop a board so that it stood upright in the water and did not move appreciably. A line with knots separated by a known distance was attached to the board. To keep track of the distance the ship traveled, a sailor counted these knots as he let the line out overboard.

Meanwhile, as the line fell into the sea, a sandglass was used to measure time. From the distance and time measurements, it was a simple matter to calculate the ship's speed. Knowing the speed of the ship and its direction of travel, a navigator could plot the ship's path.

Unfortunately, the sandglasses were not very accurate timers, and navigators were often surprised when they spied land known to be far east or west of where they thought they were. Accurate pendulum clocks became available after 1657, but such clocks were useless on a ship rolling and pitching at sea.

In 1707, an English fleet was wrecked because of incorrect assumptions about its longitude. Seven years later, the British government established a Board of Longitude empowered to present a prize of £20,000 to whoever could build a device that would allow navigators to establish their longitude accurately. In 1763, John Harrison was awarded the prize for his spring-driven No. 4 Marine Chronometer. Harrison's timepiece lost less than 2 minutes in 147 days.

Near the beginning of the twentieth century, navigators could rely on time signals sent by radio around the world. Today a "beep" establishing an exact time can be heard on almost any radio station. The first such signal was sent from the Boston Navy Yard on August 9, 1905.

Navigators on modern ships establish both their latitude and longitude based on radio signals from satellites. The NAVSTAR global positioning system (GPS) consists of a number of satellites in orbits around the earth's poles at altitudes of more than 16,000 kilometers (10,000 mi). These satellites transmit radio signals that can be picked up by a receiver on the ship. Each signal is sent at a very precise moment in time. The time it

John Harrison's No. 4 Marine Chronometer was the first timepiece that allowed navigators to establish longitude accurately. A replica of the spring-driven watch is shown here.

takes the signal to reach the ship establishes the distance of the ship from the satellite; radio signals travel at an unvarying speed—the speed of light, 300,000 km/s (186,000 mi/s).

This distance alone does not give the position of

the ship, however. As you can see in Figure 28, the ship could be anywhere along a circle A that has the satellite at its center. A signal from a second satellite establishes a second circle, B, on which the ship could be located. The ship must be at one of the two points, P_1 or P_2, where the two circles intersect. A third signal from yet another satellite finally defines the ship's position since three circles, A, B, and C, can intersect at only one point—P_1 in this case.

Because the time intervals can be measured to tenths of microseconds (10^{-7} s), the position of the ship can be calculated very accurately—to within a few meters of the true location. A computer connected to the receiver quickly performs the calculations and displays them on a screen.

ELECTRIC CLOCKS

With the arrival of electric power in the early twentieth century, a new way to regulate clocks became available. Power companies in the United States transmit electricity as 60-Hz alternating current, which means the current alternates from positive to negative and back 60 times a second. Synchronous electric motors, which turn at the same rate as the oscillating current, could thus replace springs, pendulums, and other escapement mechanisms. These clock motors swing exactly 60 times each second or 5,184,000 times every day. By 1940, half the clocks sold in the United States were electric.

During the 1920s, several observatories built very sophisticated clocks powered by electricity. They had pendulums that periodically received energy from an

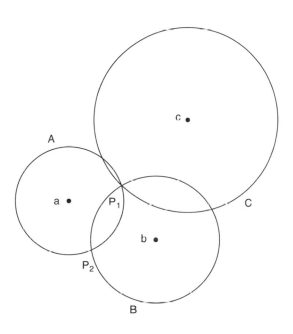

Figure 28. The global positioning system (GPS) has a number of satellites in orbits around the Earth to help ships and other vehicles determine their position. For example, a ship would receive radio signals from three satellites at positions a, b, and c, above. At precise times, the satellites send out signal pulses that travel outward in all directions. Because the signals travel at the same speed through space, the time each one arrives at the ship is a measure of the ship's distance from the sending satellite. These distances for each of the three satellites are outlined by circles A, B, and C. The point, P_1, where the circles intersect, is the position of the ship.

electrical source. These clocks were accurate to a fraction of a second in a year, which has a total of 31,557,600 seconds.

THE QUARTZ CLOCK

Quartz clocks were developed in 1929. Quartz, a type of crystal, has the unusual property of producing an electric voltage when it is put under pressure. In simple terms, if you squeeze a quartz crystal, it acts like a battery. The response of a crystal to pressure is called the *piezoelectric effect*. Conversely, if a voltage is applied to the crystal, it moves. A varying voltage causes the crystal to vibrate at a frequency that depends on its dimensions. This frequency, its *natural frequency,* does not change.

Researchers found that a crystal vibrating in this way could control the oscillation of an electric current and regulate a timepiece. By the beginning of World War II, quartz clocks were being manufactured with an accuracy of 6 seconds in 100,000,000,000 seconds, 0.002 second per year, or 1 second in 500 years. Quartz wristwatches became available in 1969, with the advent of microelectronics.

A quartz watch is any watch regulated by a crystal vibrating as a result of the piezoelectric effect. Because the crystal vibrates at a very high frequency, watchmakers had to devise mechanisms to convert the frequency to a value suitable for turning the hands of a watch. In fact, most of the parts found under a watch's back cover are there to reduce the frequency of the timing oscillations.

The tiny "arms" of the crystal, which is cut in the form of a miniature tuning fork as in Figure 29a, vibrate at about 30 kilohertz: 30,000 times per second. An integrated circuit (IC) chip contains devices that successively divide the frequency by 2. This requires that the frequency of the tuning fork be a power of 2. Therefore, the crystal is cut so that its frequency is 2^{15} or 32,768 Hz.

The IC produces pulses at precise 1-second intervals. These pulses drive the watch's motor, causing it to rotate 180 degrees with each pulse. Because it makes rotations in steps, this kind of motor is called a *stepping motor*. Its operation is illustrated in Figure 29. The rest of the mechanism is similar to a conventional watch. The shaft of the motor is connected to gears that cause the second, minute, and hour hands to rotate at relative rates in ratios of 720:12:1, respectively.

ATOMIC CLOCKS

The most accurate clocks in the world today are atomic clocks. These clocks have no face, hands, or readout. Yet they are the reference standard for calibrating the world's clocks. Tracking time according to events that take place on the atomic level, these clocks are accurate to 1 second in 300,000 years. The GPS satellites described earlier use atomic clocks to provide the very accurate time intervals required to establish longitude and latitude to within a few meters.

In atomic clocks, the atoms serve the same purpose as did pendulums or quartz crystals in earlier clocks. Most atomic clocks use cesium atoms, which,

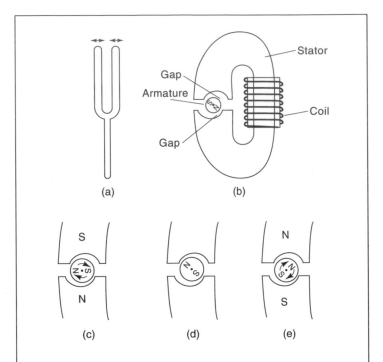

(a)   (b)

(c)   (d)   (e)

Figure 29. (a) The quartz crystal inside a watch is shaped like a tuning fork. It vibrates in response to an electric voltage from a battery. (b) The vibrations are processed to produce pulses that drive a stepping motor, which has a cross section as shown. The armature is a permanent magnet that can rotate freely. But because it is attracted to the soft iron of the stator, it is normally positioned with poles at the smallest gap between stator and armature. (c) When a current pulse flows in the coil, the stator becomes magnetized. The poles across each gap repel each other because they are the same polarity, and the armature turns. (d) When the current stops, the armature keeps going until opposite poles are across the gap from each other. This occurs at approximately 180° from the previous position. (e) The next current pulse reverses the polarity of the stator and pushes the armature through its next step.

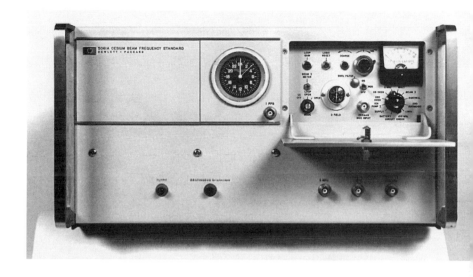

The cesium atomic clock is the most accurate clock in the world today. Its timing is regulated according to the energy emitted by cesium atoms.

like all atoms, are quantized. This means that the atoms have discrete energy levels. At its lowest energy level, called its ground state, an atom might have an energy of E_1. At higher energy levels it has energies of E_2, E_3, E_4, etc. But the atom never has an amount of energy that lies between these values. Thus, an atom in its ground state can accept a quantity of energy equal to $E_2 - E_1$, $E_3 - E_1$, $E_4 - E_1$, $E_3 - E_2$, $E_4 - E_3$, $E_4 - E_2$. . . .

When energy is emitted by an atom, it is in the form of electromagnetic radiation, such as light. If the frequency of the emitted radiation lies between 4.3×10^{14} and 7.5×10^{14} Hz, it is visible light. Higher frequencies would be in the form of ultraviolet light, lower frequencies might appear as infrared light or micro-waves. The higher the frequency of the radiation, the greater its energy. Thus, the frequency of radiation emitted by the atom is a measure of the energy it is releasing.

As atoms oscillate between two energy states they emit and absorb energy at very stable frequencies. Such stable frequencies make ideal standards because they are not affected by other variable factors such as temperature, air pressure, or gravity. In most atomic clocks, the energy absorbed or released is the result of transitions between so-called hyperfine energy levels—energy levels that are close together and that result from magnetic forces due to the spin of electrons within the atoms.

Figure 30 illustrates the operation of a cesium clock. A beam of cesium atoms emerges from a heated chamber in a vacuum. A magnetic "filter" allows only those atoms with the proper energy to pass. The others are bent in such a way by the magnetic field that they do not enter the microwave cavity. Inside the cavity, microwave photons of a particular frequency (9,192 megahertz) bombard the atoms. The frequency is such that a photon has just enough energy to raise the energy of a cesium atom to the next hyperfine level.

Energized atoms emerging from the microwave cavity pass through another field filter. Only those atoms with the correct amount of energy are bent along a path that leads to a detector. The detector, which is a hot wire, ionizes the cesium atoms that strike it. The electrons released when the atoms ionize produce an electric current. The current in the detector will be a maximum when the frequency of the microwaves in the cavity matches the natural frequency associated with

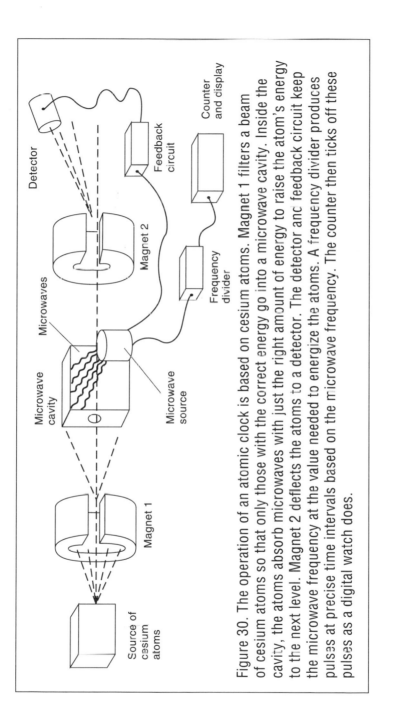

Figure 30. The operation of an atomic clock is based on cesium atoms. Magnet 1 filters a beam of cesium atoms so that only those with the correct energy go into a microwave cavity. Inside the cavity, the atoms absorb microwaves with just the right amount of energy to raise the atom's energy to the next level. Magnet 2 deflects the atoms to a detector. The detector and feedback circuit keep the microwave frequency at the value needed to energize the atoms. A frequency divider produces pulses at precise time intervals based on the microwave frequency. The counter then ticks off these pulses as a digital watch does.

the energy difference between two hyperfine levels. A feedback system keeps the current at a maximum. Should the current decrease, the feedback system adjusts the frequency of the microwaves in the cavity until the current is again at a maximum.

It is the microwave frequency that provides a measure of time. A frequency divider coupled to the microwave source produces pulses separated by precisely equal intervals of time. These pulses can be used to calibrate other clocks. The microwaves acting on the atoms have a similar function to the varying voltage that causes a quartz crystal to oscillate at a particular frequency in a quartz watch.

In 1967, the cesium clock became the world standard for time. One second was redefined to be 9,192,631,770 periods or wavelengths of radiation emitted by the cesium-133 atom. Although cesium clocks are very accurate, research indicates that future clocks will be even better.

Today, International Atomic Time, based on cesium clocks, is periodically compared with mean solar time, our clock time, after it has been corrected for the effects of the precession of the Earth's axis. As soon as the two deviate by more than 0.9 s, a "leap second" is added to the corrected mean solar time. Between 1972 and 1990, 15 leap seconds were added.

TIME
AND
VELOCITY

Time allows us to measure the passage of events in our lives and in history. But time also helps us determine rates. We must know the time period over which money is to be paid to prepare interest rates, for instance. We can calculate speed by dividing the distance traveled by the time in transit. We can even divide by time twice to measure acceleration—the rate at which speed changes.

In this chapter, you will learn how rates are calculated and used. You will also learn that Isaac Newton's concept of time as an endless, steady flow independent of all else was found to be wanting. Time, Albert Einstein found, depends on velocity.

TIME, DISTANCE, SPEED, AND VELOCITY

People often use time as a measure of distance. You have probably heard people say, "We're 2 hours from home." What they mean is that if they continue to travel at a certain speed, they will reach home in 2 hours. Distance traveled can be found by multiplying speed by time. For example, if you maintain a speed of 50 mph (80 kmph) for 2 hours, you will travel 100 miles (160 km) :

$$50 \text{ miles/hour} \times 2 \text{ hours} = 100 \text{ miles.}$$

Notice that the hours units cancel out because hours/hour = 1. Whether or not you reach home in 2 hours depends on the direction you go. If you make a wrong turn, you may travel 100 miles and still be 2 hours from home.

Many people think that *speed* and *velocity* have the same meaning, but, in fact, they do not. *Speed* is what you might read on a speedometer. It tells you only how fast you are going—15 mph (24 kmph), 60 mph (96 kmph), and so on. If you are in a car that has a compass as well as a speedometer, you can determine your velocity. *Velocity* measures direction as well as a magnitude. For example, if your speedometer reads 30 mph and your compass indicates that you are traveling due south, then your velocity is 30 mph south. Other velocities might be 60 kmph at 30° east of north or, if you are running a race, 8.5 m/s at 40° north of west.

Project 19

In Chapter 5 you learned that the NAVSTAR GPS system can synchronize signals from different satellites to within a tenth of a microsecond (10^{-7} s). Show that with this accuracy, position can be established to within 30 m. The speed of radio sig-

nals is the same as the speed of light: 300,000,000 m/s (3.0 × 10⁸ m/s).

Speed and velocity are both *rates*: that is, they measure distance traveled with respect to (divided by) time. For example, 50 miles per hour can be written

50 miles/1hour, or
100 miles/2 hours

Rates are not limited to speed or velocity. People are often paid an hourly rate. For example, you might get a job that pays $10/hour. This means that your employer will pay you $10 for every hour you work. A secretary's rate of pay might be based on his or her typing rate, which can be measured in words per minute. The production rate at an automobile factory might be measured in cars per day. How many other examples of rates can you think of?

Investigation 23: Speed and Velocity

Find a safe location overlooking a highway with posts, lines, trees, or other features that can be used as markers. As a car passes a marker in front of you, signal a friend in front of a marker down the road to start a stopwatch. When the car passes the marker down the road, your friend should stop the watch. If you know the distance between the markers and the time it took the car to travel that distance, how can you calculate the car's speed?

If the speed you calculate is in meters per second or feet per second, how can you convert it to miles per hour or kilometers per hour? What additional information do you need to determine a car's *velocity*?

If you know the distance between the markers, how can you make a table that will tell you a car's speed once you know its time between markers? Were any of the cars traveling over the speed limit?

RATES OF RATES

We define the *rate* at which we travel as speed or velocity (if we know the direction). But a rate can also change with time. For example, a car starts from rest. Its initial speed is zero. Suppose that its speed increases at a uniform rate, say by 5 mph every second, until it reaches 50 mph. It then maintains this speed for at least the next 60 seconds. While the car's speed is increasing, we say it is *accelerating*. Its *speed*, which is the rate at which distance changes with time, is increasing with time. Consequently, we can measure the change in the car's speed with time, which is its distance per unit time per unit time (distance/time/time). The best way to see this is to make a graph of the car's speed as a function of time as shown in Figure 31.

The initial slope of the graph reveals the car's acceleration. It shows that the speed increases from 0 to 50 mph (80 kmph) in 10 seconds. The slope, which is equal to the rise over the run, is

$$\frac{50 \text{ mph} - 0 \text{ mph}}{10 \text{ s} - 0 \text{ s}} = 5 \text{ mph/s}$$

You get the same value if you take a shorter segment of the graph. Notice the small triangle formed by dashed lines in Figure 31, where

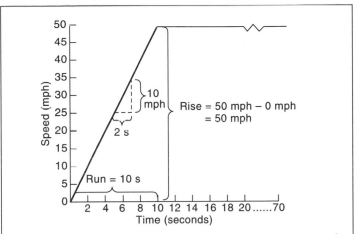

Figure 31. A car starts from rest and increases its speed at a rate of 5 mph/s for a period of 10 seconds. After 10 seconds of acceleration, it maintains its speed of 50 mph for at least one minute.

$$\frac{\text{rise}}{\text{run}} = \frac{35\text{ mph} - 25\text{ mph}}{7\text{ s} - 5\text{ s}} = \frac{10\text{ mph}}{2\text{ s}} = 5\text{ mph/s}.$$

In general, you see that the change in speed, which can be written as Δv, divided by the change in time, Δt, gives the acceleration, a. That is,

$$a = \frac{\Delta v}{\Delta t}.$$

But remember, speed is a rate too. We define speed or velocity as

$$v = \Delta d/\Delta t \text{ or } v = \frac{\Delta d}{\Delta t}$$

133

Consequently, we might write our equation for acceleration as

$$a = \frac{\Delta v}{\Delta t}, \text{ or } a = \frac{\Delta(\Delta d/\Delta t)}{\Delta t}$$

During the period from 10 to 70 seconds, the car's speed does not change. Its acceleration, therefore, is zero, or, if you prefer, the rate of change of speed is zero: $\Delta v/\Delta t = 0$ because $\Delta v = 0$.

During that same interval, the car traveled a distance of 0.83 mile because for constant velocity

$d = v \times t = 50$ mi/h x 60 s $= 50$ mi/h $\times$ (60/3,600) h $= 0.83$ mi.

As you may have noticed, 0.83 mile is equal to the rectangular area under the graph from 10 to 70 seconds. The length of the rectangle is 60 s, or, since there are 3,600 seconds in an hour, 60/3,600h; its height is 50 mi/h; the area, which is the product of the length and the height, is, therefore

50 mi/h $\times$ 60/3,600 h $= 0.83$ mi.

You can find the distance the car traveled in the first ten seconds in the same way; that is, find the area under the graph from 0 to 10 s. If you remember that the area of a triangle is one-half the base times the height, you should have no difficulty.

Project 20

In Figure 31, how far did the car travel during the first 10 seconds? How far did it travel during the entire 70-second period shown in the graph?

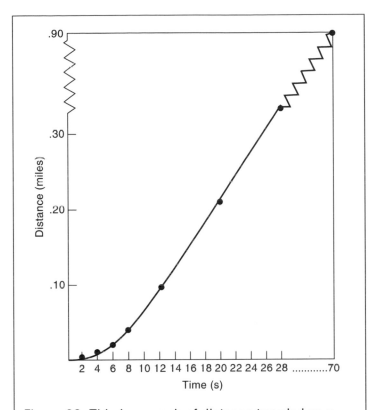

Figure 32. This is a graph of distance traveled as a function of time for the car whose speed versus time was plotted in Figure 31. Notice that the slope (distance/time) is constant only when the speed is constant. The slope increases during the time that the car is accelerating because speed (distance/time) is increasing with time.

Figure 32 is a graph of the *distance* the car traveled as a function of time. How does the total distance traveled in 70 seconds compare with the value you found in Project 20? Why does the slope of the graph in

Figure 32 increase between 0 and 10 seconds? Why does the slope remain constant from 10 to 70 seconds?

Acceleration is always expressed in units of distance divided by time divided by time—or distance divided by time squared. If velocity is measured in miles per hour and time in seconds, then the units of acceleration are mph/s. But if the velocity is measured in kilometers per seconds, as is often true of space vehicles, then the acceleration is expressed as km/s/s or km/s^2. The units km/s/s and km/s^2 are equivalent because

$$km/s/s = km/s \times 1/s = km/s^2.$$

Project 21

All falling bodies accelerate at the same uniform rate if air resistance is negligible. Table 4 shows the velocity of a falling object at various points in time after its release. Use the data in the table to

TABLE 4: Velocity of a Falling Object	
Velocity (m/s)	**Time after Release (s)**
1.0	0.10
2.0	0.20
2.9	0.30
3.9	0.40
4.9	0.50
5.9	0.60
6.8	0.70
7.8	0.80
8.8	0.90
9.8	1.00

This photograph shows a billiard ball as it falls next to a meter stick in a dark room. You can see the position of the ball every 1/30 second, thanks to a strobe light that was flashed at that frequency. What can you tell about the ball's velocity from just looking at the photograph?

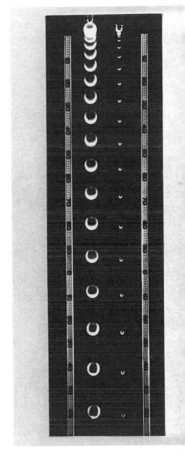

plot a graph of velocity as a function of time for the falling object.

What is the acceleration of the object? How far did it fall during the time shown on the graph? What do you think its velocity would be after 1.20 seconds?

Use the photograph of a falling billiard ball to determine the ball's acceleration. How closely do your results agree with the value you found from the graph of the data in Table 4?

Project 22

With a strobe light and camera, photograph a moving object such as a toy train running along a *straight track. Mount a flashlight bulb on the object to mark a point on it. How can you use the data to determine the object's speed?*

Use the same equipment to photograph a falling object. What is the acceleration of the object according to your data?

Investigation 24: Reaction Time

In any sport, reaction time—the time required to respond to a stimulus—is a key to an athlete's success. A tennis player must respond quickly to his or her opponent's serve. A batter has less than half a second to react to a pitch once the ball leaves the pitcher's hand. The success of an offensive football team depends to a great extent on its quick response to the quarterback's starting signal, while the defensive team must react quickly to the initial movement of the ball.

How quickly can you respond to a command? To find out, you can measure reaction time with a meter stick or a yardstick. Have a friend hold a meter stick or yardstick so that its lower end is even with your extended forefinger and thumb as shown in Figure 33. To prevent yourself from anticipating when your friend is about to release the stick, close your eyes or wear a blindfold. Your friend should say, "Go!" at the moment he or she releases the stick. You react to the signal by bringing your thumb and fingers together to catch the falling yardstick or meter stick.

The distance the stick falls before you catch it is a measure of your reaction time. If you did Project 21, you found that falling objects accelerate at a rate of 9.8 m/s² (32 ft/s²). Knowing this acceleration and the dis-

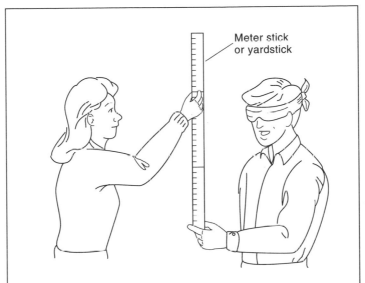

Figure 33. Measure your reaction time by catching a measuring stick as quickly as possible after it is released.

tance the measuring stick fell, you can calculate the time using the equations in Figure 34. Table 5 lists the reaction times for certain distances the stick might fall. If you need more data for distance and time, you can copy Table 5 into your notebook and add to it with your calculations.

Make four or five runs of the reaction-time experiment and average the results. What was your reaction time? What is your partner's reaction time?

Measure the reaction times of a variety of people. Does reaction time appear to be related to a person's age? Sex? Occupation? Athletic skill? Height? Weight? Other factors?

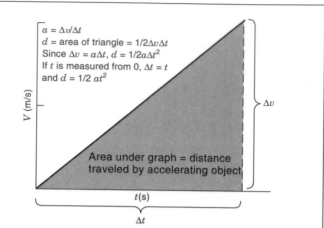

$a = \Delta v/\Delta t$
d = area of triangle = $1/2\Delta v\Delta t$
Since $\Delta v = a\Delta t$, $d = 1/2a\Delta t^2$
If t is measured from 0, $\Delta t = t$
and $d = 1/2\ at^2$

Δv

V (m/s)

Area under graph = distance
traveled by accelerating object

t(s)

Δt

Figure 34. As you can see from this graph of velocity versus time for a body that is accelerating uniformly, the acceleration is the slope of the graph ($\Delta v/\Delta t$). The distance the object travels is equal to the area under the graph. For a falling body, $\Delta v/\Delta t$ = 9.8 m/s^2 when $\Delta t = 1.0$ s.

TABLE 5: Reaction Times Based on the Distance a Measuring Stick Falls

Distance (cm)	Time (s)	Distance (in)	Time (s)
5.0	0.10	2.0	0.10
10	0.14	4.0	0.14
15	0.17	6.0	0.18
20	0.20	8.0	0.20
25	0.23	10.0	0.23
30	0.25	12.0	0.25

Project 23

The photograph shows a bullet after it has passed through an apple. The bullet is traveling at about 1,000 m/s (3,280 ft/s). Since the bullet appears to

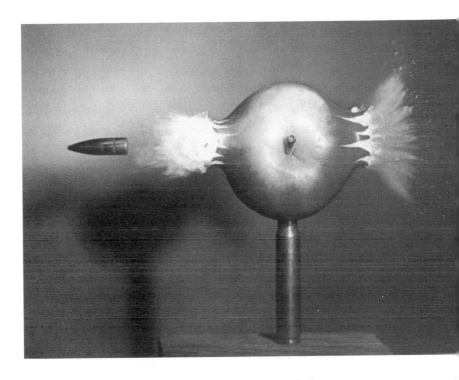

The bullet to the left just shot through the apple at 1,000 m/s. What must the exposure time have been for the photograph?

be almost stationary, what do you estimate was the exposure time for the photograph?

Project 24

You have probably seen slow-motion movies. How are they made? What is done to slow the motion? If possible, make your own slow-motion movie. If the athletic department at your school has the equipment you need, find out whether you may borrow it for this project.

EINSTEIN AND RELATIVITY

In 1905, Albert Einstein published his special theory of relativity and changed our concept of time forever. His theory led to the conclusion that the perception of time is relative: that is, the rate at which time goes by is different for two people who are moving with respect to each other. The greater their relative speed, the greater the difference in their measurement of time. But the difference becomes significant only when the relative velocity is on the order of the speed of light.

This concept of time resulted from a tenet of Einstein's special theory of relativity. It states that the speed of light in space is the same for all observers. In other words, no matter what the frame of reference, or point of view from which a person is watching, the speed of light is always the same. Before seeing how this leads to relative time, let's look at how scientists proved Einstein's tenet correct.

Before Einstein developed his theory, Albert Michelson had measured the speed of light very accurately and found it to be very nearly 300,000 km/s (186,000 mi/s). Michelson, together with Edward Morley, later performed careful experiments that showed that the speed of light is the same no matter which direction it travels. That may not sound like a remarkable result, but it surprised most scientists at the time.

They were surprised because they believed that light waves travel on a material called *ether*, just as sound waves travel on air. Since light, unlike sound, can be transmitted through airless outer space, scientists had invented an invisible ether to explain the transmission of light. They believed that the ether permeated all space and served as the medium through which light moved at the incredibly high velocity measured by Michelson.

If the ether existed, then the Earth must move through it as a swimmer moves through water. Light traveling on the Earth, then, would be affected by the relative motion of the ether. The velocity of the light can be expected to be slightly different when it travels parallel to the direction the Earth is moving than when it travels perpendicular to that direction.

To see why, consider two identical boats on a river as shown in Figure 35. In Figure 35a, a boat moves 5 km downstream and returns upstream to its starting position. The second boat, in Figure 35b, crosses the stream heading perpendicular to the current and returns heading 180° from its original direction. The boats have identical motors, which, in still water, give them a velocity of 10 kmph. The stream is 5 km wide and has a current of 5 kmph.

The round-trip time for the boat that goes downstream and back is 1.33 hours or 80 minutes. Its downstream velocity is 15 kmph − 10 kmph from the motor + 5 kmph from the current. It takes 0.33 hour, or 20 minutes, to travel 5 km at 15 kmph.

$$\frac{5 \text{ km}}{15 \text{ km/h}} = 0.33\text{h}.$$

Its return trip is much slower because it is opposed by a 5-kmph current. Its upstream velocity is only 5 kmph (10 kmph − 5 kmph). Consequently, it takes 1 hour to travel the 5 km back to its starting point.

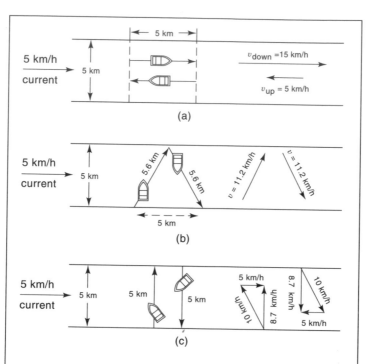

Figure 35. A boat travels upstream and downstream at different speeds than across a stream. (a) A boat with a speed of 10 kmph in still water travels 5 km downstream at 15 kmph and 5 km upstream at 5 kmph. Its round-trip time will be 1.33 h. (b) An identical boat going across the stream travels 11.2 km on its round trip because it is carried 5 km downstream by the current; the trip takes 1 hour. (c) If the boat's bow is pointed 30° upstream, it travels a total of 10 km. Its average speed is 8.7 kmph so it takes 1.15 h to make the round trip.

The boat in Figure 35b travels across the stream and back in 1 hour (5 km + 5 km, both at 10 km/h). Of course, it winds up downstream because the current carries it 5 km downstream in 1 hour, and its total path

144

covers 11.2 km, which means it had an average velocity of 11.2 km/h in the directions shown in the diagram. Although the two boats were traveling at the same speed, this boat took only 1 hour to cover more than the distance it took the first boat 80 minutes to traverse.

What if the boat's bow is pointed upstream at 30° to compensate for the current? Then it would move straight across the river, perpendicular to the current as in Figure 35c. Even so, its time for the round trip will be different from the time of the boat that moves downstream and back. The velocity in a direction perpendicular to the stream will now be 8.7 km/h. Therefore, the time to make the 10-km trip over and back will be

$$\frac{10 \text{ km}}{8.7 \text{ km/h}} = 1.15\text{h}.$$

The two boats took different times to travel the same distance; consequently, their average speed must have been different. Similarly, if light on a moving Earth (the boat in the analogy) passes through an ether (the river in the analogy), it would be expected that the light would move faster in a direction perpendicular to the Earth's motion than in a direction parallel to the Earth's path. But, in fact, Michelson and Morley found no difference; the speed of light was the same in all directions.

Finding such results unbelievable, many other scientists repeated Michelson and Morley's experiment with various modifications. All the results confirmed the original experiment—the speed of light is constant in all directions. Thus, they confirmed Einstein's special relativity theory.

TIME AND RELATIVITY

The constancy of the speed of light led Einstein to some startling conclusions about time. Most of his experiments were thought experiments in which he imagined a hypothetical situation and drew logical conclusions from it. Here's one of his thought experiments: Consider a spaceship traveling close to the speed of light above the Earth. An astronaut onboard the ship carries out an experiment to measure the speed of light. She directs a beam of light from the ceiling to a mirror on the floor, as shown in Figure 36a, and measures the time it takes the light to travel to the mirror and back. The time interval is very small, to be sure, but we assume it can be measured with atomic clocks. The velocity is equal to $2d/t$ and

$$2d/t = 300,000 \text{ km/s.}$$

A scientist on Earth obtained the same results when he performed the experiment on the ground. He now observes from Earth the experiment as it is performed in the spaceship, which is transparent. Because the spaceship is moving relative to him, the light actually travels along the path shown in Figure 36b. This distance is $2L$. Since $2L$ is greater than $2d$, the time, t', must be greater than t because the speed of light is constant. He finds the speed of light to be

$$2L/t' = 300,000 \text{ km/s.}$$

To the observer on Earth, the astronaut's clock has measured a time interval t', even though the clock itself reads t. The astronaut's clock appears to run too slowly compared to the clock on Earth.

146

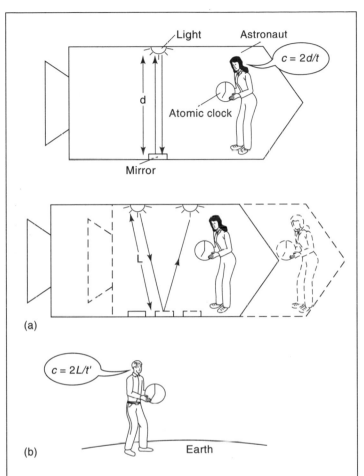

(a)

(b)

Figure 36. This thought experiment shows that time is relative. (a) An astronaut in a fast-moving spaceship measures the speed of light and finds it to be $2d/t$. (b) A person on Earth, who has done the same experiment and obtained the same results, observes the experiment in the spaceship. Because the spaceship is moving relative to the Earth, the earthbound observer sees the light travel a distance $2L$ in a time t'. From the observer's point of view, the clock on the spaceship runs slower than an identical one on Earth.

Einstein showed mathematically that moving clocks do, in fact, run slower from the viewpoint of a stationary observer. Of course, from the astronaut's point of view, her clock is stationary; it is the Earth clock that is running too slowly. For any two observers, where one is moving at a velocity v relative to the other, the moving observer's clock will appear to "tick" more slowly. In fact, you can calculate how much more slowly with the following equation of Einstein's:

$$t' = \frac{t}{\sqrt{1 - v^2/c^2}},$$

where t is a time interval measured by a clock at rest, t' is the time interval measured by a moving clock, c is the speed of light, and v is the speed of the moving clock relative to the stationary one.

As you can see, because c is very large, t and t' are virtually the same when objects move relative to each other at ordinary speeds. Even at one-tenth the speed of light (30,000 km/s or 18,600 mi/s), a moving clock's apparent time is increased by a factor of only 1.005, as the following calculation shows:

$$t' = \frac{t}{\sqrt{1 - v^2/c^2}} = \frac{t}{\sqrt{1 - 0.1^2/1.0^2}} = \frac{t}{\sqrt{1 - 0.01}} = 1.005t$$

A clock that ticks every second when at rest will tick every 1.005 s when moving at $0.1c$.

Project 25

A stationary observer measures a time t on her clock. Calculate the apparent time interval indi-

cated on a clock that is moving relative to her at a velocity of 0.5c, 0.9c, and 0.99c.

Investigation 25: Measuring the Speed of Sound

Because light travels so swiftly, its speed is not easily measured. It took Michelson years to build and set up the equipment he used to determine the speed of light with good accuracy. Today, it is possible to measure the speed of light in a high school laboratory, but the equipment is expensive. You can, however, measure the speed of sound quite easily.

If you've ever been to a baseball game, you've probably already observed that the speed of sound is much less than the speed of light. When seated far from home plate, you can see the ball hit the bat well before you *hear* the sound made by their collision. Because the light needed to see the collision reaches you before the sound, you know that the speed of light exceeds the speed of sound.

You can make a rough estimate of the speed of sound by standing as far as possible from a friend who makes a loud sound. Have the friend strike a board or some other object with a bat or a hammer. The sight of the event should be almost instantaneous; even at a distance of 1 km, the reflected light would take only 0.0000033 second to reach you. At the moment you see the bat hit the object, start a stopwatch. Stop the watch when you hear the sound. Now how can you determine the speed of sound? To see how accurate your measurements are, repeat the experiment several times.

To make a more accurate measurement of the speed of sound, stand about 50 m (164 ft) from a large wall or some other large vertical surface such as the side of a metal, concrete, or brick building. Make a loud, sharp sound with a pair of boards or a loud clicker, such as a "cricket." Slam the boards together or snap the clicker and listen for the echo from the wall. The echo indicates that sound was reflected by the wall.

The time interval between the sound and its echo is too short to measure accurately with a stopwatch. But you can measure the time it takes to make 20 to 40 claps or clicks if you adjust the rate of clapping or clicking until each clap or click coincides with the echo of the sound that preceded it. Keep the rate of sounds and echoes simultaneous for ten seconds or longer, and have your partner use a stopwatch to measure the time it takes you to make a specific number of claps or clicks. The time between each clip is the time it takes the sound to make one round trip from you to the wall and back.

Suppose you are standing 50 m from the wall and you find it takes 10.0 s for you to make 35 clicks that coincide with their echoes. From these measurements, you can calculate the speed of sound as follows:

The distance traveled in one round trip is:

$$2 \times 50 \text{ m} = 100 \text{ m } (328 \text{ ft}).$$

The time for one round trip is:

$$10.0 \text{ s}/34 = 0.29 \text{ s}.$$

The speed of sound then is found by:

$$\text{speed} = \text{distance/time} = 100 \text{ m}/0.29 \text{ s} = 340 \text{ m/s or } 1{,}100 \text{ ft/s}.$$

What do you find the speed of sound to be? Repeat your measurements several times. Are your results reasonably consistent? Are the data in the example given comparable to your data?

How can you check to be sure that the speed of sound does not change with the distance it travels? Does the speed of sound vary with temperature?

Project 26

If your school has the equipment needed to measure the speed of light, set up the apparatus and determine the speed of light for yourself. The necessary equipment is an optics bench, lenses, a laser with an aligning bench, a rotating mirror, a measuring microscope with a beam splitter, and a good light source.

EXPERIMENTAL TESTS OF RELATIVITY

As you might expect, this discussion of relativity has been limited to the way it has affected our notions of time, but Einstein's theory was much broader in scope. It changed our entire view of the universe, of space and gravity, as well as time. The consequences of Einstein's theory, like those of any theory, have been tested experimentally, and the theory has come through with flying colors.

With the development of atomic clocks, it became possible to compare the time kept by clocks on fast-moving jet airplanes and satellites with clocks at rest on the Earth. Although even the speed of satellites is small compared with the speed of light, atomic clocks on board such vehicles have been shown to run more slowly than those on Earth. In fact, the NAVSTAR GPS discussed in Chapter 5 must take into account the reduced ticking rate of clocks on their satellites in order to provide accurate navigational information.

Even before atomic clocks were mounted on satellites, physicists had tested relativity with *muons*—particles produced in the upper atmosphere when cosmic rays strike atoms of air. These muons rapidly decay into other particles. In fact, the *half-life* of muons—the time required for half of them to decay—is only 1.5 microseconds (1.5 millionths of a second). In the upper atmosphere, they travel toward Earth at 97 percent of the speed of light ($0.97c$). At this speed, we would expect their "clocks" to tick only about one-fourth as fast as clocks on Earth.

By measuring the fraction of these fast-moving muons that reach Earth before decaying, it was found that their "clocks" do indeed slow down from our perspective. Over a period of 6.0 microseconds, we would expect only about 63 of every 1,000 muons to reach Earth if their clocks did not slow down. That number comes from knowing that the time period is equal to four half-lives; only 1/16 ($^1/_2 \times {}^1/_2 \times {}^1/_2 \times {}^1/_2$) of the muons would be expected to exist at the end of the period. But if their clocks run one-fourth as fast as ours, only one half-life would have transpired in 6.0 microseconds. Therefore, according to Einstein's theory of relativity, half of the muons should remain upon reaching Earth. Indeed, experiments found that about 500 of 1,000 muons reached the Earth. Einstein's theory was confirmed.

The theory of relativity drastically changed our concept of time. Your clock and my clock, even though synchronized initially, may not continue to agree. If you take off in a spaceship that travels at very high speeds, your clock will tick slower than mine. But Einstein's theory also changed our concept of space. To him space and time are united to make up what he called space-time. Time becomes the fourth dimension.

A fourth dimension is difficult to envision because we live in a three-dimensional world. We can easily see two dimensions; for example, the graph of distance versus time in Figure 32 represents two dimensions. It gives an object's position along a line, or one spatial dimension, as a function of time—another dimension. By adding a third axis, we could plot an object's position on a surface as a function of time; that would be a three-dimensional representation. But we can't plot an object's position in space as a function of time because we can see only three axes in the physical world. The only way to investigate a fourth dimension is by mathematical means.

The strange nature of time may be hard to grasp at first. If this book has stirred your interest in the ongoing quest to understand time, you may want to pursue the mathematics required to thoroughly comprehend the theory of relativity. If your mathematical skills, like those of most people, are not up to so ambitious a task, you can explore the subject further by reading some of the books in For Further Reading. Take some time to learn more about the exotic dimension of time.

APPENDIX:
SCIENCE SUPPLY COMPANIES

Carolina Biological Supply Co.
   2700 York Road
   Burlington, NC 27215
   (910) 584-0381
Central Scientific Co. (CENCO)
   3300 CENCO Parkway
   Franklin Park, IL 60131
   (800) 262-3626
Connecticut Valley Biological Supply Co., Inc.
   82 Valley Road, Box 326
   Southampton, MA 01073
   (800) 628-7748
Delta Education
   P.O. Box 915
   Hudson, NH 03051-0915
   (800) 258-1302
Edmund Scientific Co.
   101 East Gloucester Pike

Barrington, NJ 08007
(609) 573-6270
Fisher Scientific Co.
485 S. Frontage Road
Burr Ridge, IL 60521
(800) 955-1177
Frey Scientific Co.
905 Hickory Lane
Mansfield, OH 44905
(800) 225-3739
Nasco Science
901 Janesville Road
Fort Atkinson, WI 53538-0901
(800) 558-9595
Schoolmasters Science
745 State Circle
P.O. Box 1941
Ann Arbor, MI 48106
(313) 761-5072
Science Kit & Boreal Laboratories
777 East Park Drive,
Tonawanda, NY 14150
(800) 828-7777
Ward's Natural Science Establishment, Inc.
5100 West Henrietta Road
P.O. Box 92912
Rochester, NY 14692-9012
(800) 962-2660

FOR
FURTHER
READING

Asimov, Isaac. *Past, Present, and Future*. Buffalo: Prometheus Books, 1987.

Burns, Marilyn. *It's About Time: All You Need to Know About the Origin of Time and Calendars*. Saratoga, Calif.: R & E Publishers, 1992.

Dale, Rodney. *Timekeeping*. New York: Oxford University Press, 1992.

Ferguson, Kitty. *Black Holes in Space-Time*. New York: Watts, 1991.

Gardner, Robert. *Experimenting with Sound*. New York: Watts, 1991.

———. *Famous Experiments You Can Do*. New York: Watts, 1990.

———. *Projects in Space Science*. New York: Messner, 1988.

Jespersen, James, and Jane Fitz-Randolph. *From Sundials to Atomic Clocks: Understanding Time and Frequency*. New York: Dover.

Jones, Roger S. *Physics for the Rest of Us*. Chicago: Contemporary Books, 1992.

Kemp, Mark. "Supercool Mammals." *Discover* November 1989, p. 24.

Morrison, Philip, and Phylis Morrison. *The Ring of Truth: An Inquiry into How We Know What We Know*. New York: Random House, 1987.

Revkin, Andrew C. "Sleeping Beauties." *Discover* April 1989, pp. 62–65.

Swisher, Clarice. *Relativity: Opposing Viewpoints*. San Diego: Greenhaven Press, 1990.

Tauber, Gerald E. *Relativity: From Einstein to Black Holes*. New York: Watts, 1988.

Will, Clifford M. *Was Einstein Right? Putting General Relativity to the Test*, 2nd edition. New York: Basic Books, 1993.

Williams, Trevor J. *The History of Invention: From Stone Axes to Silicon Chips*. New York: Facts on File, 1987.

INDEX